TEXTBOOK OF GREEN BIOTECHNOLOGY

TEXTBOOK OF GREEN BIOTECHNOLOGY

Dr. Pooja
Dept. of Botany
R.C.C. College
Ghaziabad (U.P.)
(India)

DISCOVERY PUBLISHING HOUSE PVT. LTD.
NEW DELHI-110 002

Published by:
Tilak Wasan

DISCOVERY PUBLISHING HOUSE PVT. LTD.
4383/4B, Ansari Road, Darya Ganj
New Delhi-110 002 (India)
Phone : +91-11-23279245, 43596064-65
Fax : +91-11-23253475
E-mail : discoverypublishinghouse@gmail.com
sales@discoverypublishinggroup.com
web : www.discoverypublishinggroup.com

***First Edition:* 2010**

***Reprinted:* 2016**

ISBN: 978-81-8356-573-8

Textbook of Green Biotechnology

Printed at:
Infinity Imaging Systems
Delhi

Preface

Green biotechnology is biotechnology applied to agricultural processes. An example would be the selection and domestication of plants via micropropagation. Another example is the designing of transgenic plants to grow under specific environmental conditions or in the presence (or absence) of certain agricultural chemicals. One hope is that green biotechnology might produce more environmentally friendly solutions than traditional industrial agriculture. An example of this is the engineering of a plant to express a pesticide, thereby eliminating the need for external application of pesticides. An example of this would be Bt corn hether or not green biotechnology products such as this are ultimately more environmentally friendly is a topic of considerable debate.

Biotechnology is technology based on biology, especially when used in agriculture, food science, and medicine. The United Nations Convention on Biological Diversity defines biotechnology as: "Any technological application that uses biological systems, living organisms, or derivatives thereof, to make or modify products or processes for specific use".

Biotechnology is often used to refer to genetic engineering technology of the 21st century, however the term encompasses a wider range and history of procedures for modifying biological organisms according to the needs of humanity, going back to the initial modifications of native plants into improved food crops through artificial selection and hybridization. Bioengineering is the science upon which all biotechnological applications are based. With the development of new approaches and modern techniques, traditional biotechnology industries are also acquiring new horizons enabling them to improve the quality of their products and increase the productivity of their systems.

The most practical use of biotechnology, which is still present today, is the cultivation of plants to produce food suitable to humans. Agriculture has been theorized to have become the dominant way of producing food since the Neolithic Revolution. The processes and methods of agriculture have been refined by other mechanical and biological sciences since its inception. Through early biotechnology, farmers were able to select the best suited and highest-yield crops to produce enough food to support a growing population. Other uses of biotechnology were required as crops and fields became increasingly large and difficult to maintain. Specific organisms and organism by-products were used to fertilize, restore nitrogen, and control pests. Throughout the use of agriculture, farmers have inadvertently altered the genetics of their crops through introducing them to new environments and breeding them with other plants—one of the first forms of biotechnology.

Combinations of plants and other organisms were used as medications in many early civilizations. Since as early as 200 BC, people began to use disabled or minute amounts of infectious agents to immunize themselves against infections. These and similar processes have been refined in modern medicine and have led to many developments such as antibiotics, vaccines, and other methods of fighting sickness.

Using the techniques of modern biotechnology, one or two genes may be transferred to a highly developed crop variety to impart a new character that would increase its yield . However, YEA while increases in crop yield are the most obvious applications of modern biotechnology in agriculture, it is also the most difficult one. Current genetic engineering techniques work best for effects that are controlled by a single gene. Many of the genetic characteristics associated with yield (e.g., enhanced growth) are controlled by a large number of genes, each of which has a minimal effect on the overall yield. There is, therefore, much scientific work to be done in this area.

—Author

Contents

1

Introduction

'Green biotechnology' is biotechnology applied to agricultural processes. An example would be the selection and domestication of plants via micropropagation. Another example is the designing of transgenic plants to grow under specific environmental conditions or in the presence (or absence) of certain agricultural chemicals. One hope is that green biotechnology might produce more environmentally friendly solutions than traditional industrial agriculture. An example of this is the engineering of a plant to express a pesticide, thereby eliminating the need for external application of pesticides. An example of this would be Bt corn. hether or not green biotechnology products such as this are ultimately more environmentally friendly is a topic of considerable debate.

Agricultural or "green" biotechnology is being adopted at record speed around the world - in 2006, 10.3 million farmers in 22 countries cultivated genetically modified (biotech) crops on 102 million hectares. The adoption rate is seeing double-digit annual growth since 1996. Planting in India has been much slower, but is accelerating as farmers start realizing the benefits of biotech crops. In 2006, seven European countries (Portugal, Spain, Germany, France, Czech Republic, Slovakia and Romania) grew biotech crops as opposed to only one a few years ago. The number of hectares of biotech crops in Europe, although modest, is also growing significantly. The technology is safe and regulatory systems, if applied correctly in the countries of the European Union, guarantee consumers and farmers the choice of whether or not to consume and plant biotech crops.

Agricultural biotechnology offers tremendous opportunities across key European public policy goals, including innovation, education, development, health, renewable resources and energy, and trade. Biotechnology is being exploited at an accelerating rate by Europe's competitors, but if allowed to flourish, it will contribute to the increased economic and environmental sustainability of European agriculture and to efforts to ensure world food stocks keep up with rising demand.

The Benefits of Green Biotechnology

The benefits of green biotechnology to farmers, the environment, consumers and society are many. Biotech crops are able to:

- increase yields by 6%-30% on the same amount of land; thereby freeing up land for other uses than agricultural production;
- offer efficient protection against insect damage to crops; while significantly reducing the need to spray crops;
- result in permanent reductions in fuel use and resultant CO_2 emissions due to less tillage;
- have already reduced the global environmental 'foot print' of production agriculture by 14% including reductions of CO_2 emissions in 2004 equivalent to taking five million cars off the road for one year;
- produce better, safer and healthier food and feedstuffs, such as healthier vegetable oils; produce containing less harmful natural toxins such as mycotoxins;
- increase the economic viability of biofuels by reducing production costs of raw materials;
- allow farmers to grow more food more reliably in harsher climatic conditions;

- reduce water use and help us meet the Millennium Development Goals;
- protect soils from erosion and compaction through less ploughing;
- create jobs e.g. over one million new jobs were created in Argentina over a period of 10 years from the adoption of biotech crops

Implement the Biotech Crop Authorization Process

In 2001, the European Commission published a report based on 81 research projects funded by the Commission (70 million) over 15 years. The report found that biotech crops did not have "any new risks to human health or the environment beyond the usual uncertainties of conventional plant breeding. Indeed, the use of more precise technology and the greater regulatory scrutiny probably make them even safer than conventional plants and foods."

Despite the scientific findings, in 2004 the European Commission acknowledged that as far as agricultural biotechnology is concerned: ". . . Europe's position is declining as a consequence of the political inertia caused by the polarised and increasingly heated debate between opponents and advocates. ..." As a consequence of this political inertia, the stringent system for authorizing new biotech crops in the EU is not working as intended.

In spite of the fact that companies are complying with regulatory requirements and that the body responsible for scientific assessment, the European Food Safety Authority (EFSA), has issued a number of positive opinions on product safety, no product has yet been approved in the EU for cultivation since the new regulatory f ramework was adopted in 2001. In addition, approvals of products for use in animal feed and food also face undue delays in spite of positive opinions on safety from EFSA.

The approval process is not working properly for three main reasons:

1. The safety assessment part of the approval process managed by the EFSA GMO Panel is functioning very slowly.
2. The European Commission Directorates responsible for managing the approval process are not submitting proposals for decisions to the Regulatory (Member State) Committees within the times prescribed by the regulations.
3. Member State representatives at the Regulatory Committee and Council levels are not following EFSA opinions on product safety.

Suggested Solutions

1. As a matter of priority, the EFSA GMO Panel should focus its capacity on applications for product approvals, and deliver opinions in timeframes consistent with those prescribed in the regulations. Ad hoc self-tasking activities should be reduced until the backlog of applications is removed. Additional resources should be provided to EFSA to manage the increasing number of applications.
2. The European Commission should propose draft approval decisions to Member States according to their regulatory obligations with respect to legally binding timelines.
3. Member States should act in a manner consistent with their EU and International obligations, and demonstrate confidence in the regulatory process they established by making decisions on the basis of EFSA's scientific opinions.
4. The European Commission should ensure that, for biotech products authorized in the EU, Member States do not restrict farmers' access to such products through the use of arbitrary and illegal bans or through the adoption of discriminatory national or local coexistence rules.

Farmers are increasingly supporting and growing biotech crops around Europe. One group representing European farmers stated that Europe's slow adoption ". . . leaves Europe in a very uncomfortable position compared to its international competitors. Most farmers support Agriculture Commissioner Fischer Boel's statement in 2005 that ". . . Farmers should be given choice in order to reflect and adapt to the needs of the market. The decision on the use of biotech crops should be for the farmer." As the UK National Farmers Union said "... farmers should have access to technologies that have received regulatory approval and should therefore be free to choose their preferred production systems."

Public opinion is also changing. Recent polling and reports show growing support for agricultural biotech, especially where spraying of crops can be reduced or healthier food choices can be obtained. Europeans rank biotech at the bottom of the list of all concerns about foods, and a large majority of consumers says that biotech content is not important in purchasing decisionss.

Suggested Solutions

1. Societal and political leaders need to make a greater contribution towards educating citizens about the technology, its safety, its advantages and the stringent regulatory framework that is in place in Europe.
2. Europe's political leadership needs to nurture a coherence pro-growth policy that supports sustainable agriculture and is both science-based and non-discriminatory towards proven technologies.
3. Remove the uncertainties in the approvals process which only undermine citizens' confidence in European institutions and the regulatory framework.of policies and public information on green biotech

Cultivation of biotech crops is gaining momentum in the EU and has reached 65000 hectares in 2006 with 6 European countries cultivating approved biotech crops (Portugal, Spain, Germany, Czech Republic, Slovakia and France). With improvements in policies, there is great potential for further opportunities for biotech crops in the EU. However, the ambivalent position of the EU hinders such opportunities and negatively influences developing countries from the adoption of biotech crops.

In 2006, 90% of the farmers who benefited from biotech crops were resource poor farmers from developing countries, whose increased income from these crops contributed to the alleviation of poverty.

As the UN Human Development Report stated.

"Opposition in richer countries to biotech crops may set back the ability of the poorest nations to feed growing populations. . . . The world's richest nations must get over their fear of genetically engineered food if they want to help eradicate poverty in the world's poorest countries".

A number of internationally recognized reports, including the 2002 FAO report, state that agricultural biotechnology has a definite role to play in combating world hunger.

The United Nations Development Programme stated that "Biotechnology offers the only, or the best "tool of choice" for marginal ecological zones-left behind by the green revolution but home to more than half of the world's poorest people, dependent on agriculture and life stocks."

Refusals to accept food aid containing GM traces and such exemplifies the perception that Europe's perceived "ambivalent position" negatively influences developing countries in their attitude towards agricultural biotechnology.

Suggested Solutions

1. The European Union as a whole should nurture and promote coherent pro-development policy that does not discriminate promising technology.
2. At the same time, Europe's political leadership should openly communicate its support for the policies it has agreed on so as to correctly reflect the trust it has in its own regulatory system and the products approved through this system.

Biotechnology is technology based on biology, especially when used in agriculture, food science, and medicine. The United Nations Convention on Biological Diversity defines biotechnology as: "Any technological application that uses biological systems, living organisms, or derivatives thereof, to make or modify products or processes for specific use".

Biotechnology is often used to refer to genetic engineering technology of the 21st century, however the term encompasses a wider range and history of procedures for modifying biological organisms according to the needs of humanity, going back to the initial modifications of native plants into improved food crops through artificial selection and hybridization. Bioengineering is the science upon which all biotechnological applications are based. With the development of new approaches and modern techniques, traditional biotechnology industries are also acquiring new horizons enabling them to improve the quality of their products and increase the productivity of their systems.

Before 1971, the term, biotechnology, was primarily used in the food processing and agriculture industries. Since the 1970s, it began to be used by the Western scientific establishment to refer to laboratory-based techniques being developed in biological research, such as recombinant DNA or tissue culture-based processes, or horizontal gene transfer in living plants, using vectors such as the Agrobacterium bacteria to transfer DNA into a host organism. In fact, the term should be used in a much broader sense to describe the whole range of methods, both ancient and modern, used to manipulate organic materials to reach the demands of food production. So the term could be defined as, "The application of indigenous and/or scientific knowledge to the management of (parts of) microorganisms, or of cells and tissues of higher organisms, so that these supply goods and services of use to the food industry and its consumers."Biotechnology combines disciplines like genetics, molecular biology, biochemistry, embryology and cell biology, which are in turn linked to practical disciplines like chemical engineering, information technology, and robotics. Patho-biotechnology describes the exploitation of pathogens or pathogen derived compounds for beneficial effect.

The most practical use of biotechnology, which is still present today, is the cultivation of plants to produce food suitable to humans. Agriculture has been theorized to have become the dominant way of producing food since the Neolithic Revolution. The processes and methods of agriculture have been refined by other mechanical and biological sciences since its inception. Through early biotechnology, farmers were able to select the best suited and highest-yield crops to produce enough food to support a growing population. Other uses of biotechnology were required as crops and fields became increasingly large and difficult to maintain. Specific organisms and organism by-products were used to fertilize, restore nitrogen, and control pests. Throughout the use of agriculture, farmers have inadvertently altered the genetics of their crops through introducing them to new environments and breeding them with other plants—one of the first forms of biotechnology. Cultures such as those in Mesopotamia, Egypt, and Pakistan developed the process of brewing beer. It is still done by the same basic method of using malted grains (containing enzymes) to convert starch from grains into sugar and then adding specific yeasts to produce beer. In this process the carbohydrates in the grains were broken down into alcohols such as ethanol. Ancient Indians also used the juices of the plant Ephedra vulgaris and used to call it Soma. Later other cultures produced the process of Lactic acid fermentation which allowed the fermentation and preservation of other forms of food. Fermentation was also used in this time period to produce leavened bread. Although the process of fermentation was not fully understood until Louis Pasteur's work in 1857, it is still the first use of biotechnology to convert a food source into another form.

Combinations of plants and other organisms were used as medications in many early civilizations. Since as early as 200 BC, people began to use disabled or minute amounts of infectious agents to immunize themselves against infections. These and similar processes have been refined in modern medicine and have led to many developments such as antibiotics, vaccines, and other methods of fighting sickness.

In the early twentieth century scientists gained a greater understanding of microbiology and explored ways of manufacturing specific products. In 1917, Chaim Weizmann first used a pure microbiological culture in an industrial process, that of manufacturing corn starch using *Clostridium acetobutylicum* to produce acetone, which the United Kingdom desperately needed to manufacture explosives during World War I.

The field of modern biotechnology is thought to have largely begun on June 16, 1980, when the United States Supreme Court ruled that a genetically-modified microorganism could be patented in the case of *Diamond v. Chakrabarty*. Indian-born Ananda Chakrabarty, working for General Electric, had developed a bacterium (derived from the *Pseudomonas* genus) capable of breaking down crude oil, which he proposed to use in treating oil spills.

Revenue in the industry is expected to grow by 12.9% in 2008. Another factor influencing the biotechnology sector's success is improved intellectual property rights legislation—and enforcement—worldwide, as well as strengthened demand for medical and pharmaceutical products to cope with an ageing, and ailing, U.S. population.

Rising demand for biofuels is expected to be good news for the biotechnology sector, with the Department of Energy estimating ethanol usage could reduce U.S. petroleum-derived fuel consumption by up to 30% by 2030. The biotechnology sector has allowed the U.S. farming industry to rapidly increase its supply of corn and soybeans—the main inputs into biofuels—by developing genetically-modified seeds which are resistant to pests and drought. By boosting farm productivity, biotechnology plays a crucial role in ensuring that biofuel production targets are met.

Application of Biotechnology

Application of Biotechnology has applications in four major industrial areas, including health care (medical), crop production and agriculture, non food (industrial) uses of crops and other products (e.g. biodegradable plastics, vegetable oil, biofuels), and environmental uses.

For example, one application of biotechnology is the directed use of organisms for the manufacture of organic products (examples include beer and milk products). Another example is using naturally present bacteria by the mining industry in bioleaching. Biotechnology is also used to recycle, treat waste, clean up sites contaminated by industrial activities (bioremediation), and also to produce biological weapons.

A series of derived terms have been coined to identify several branches of biotechnology, for example:

- *Red biotechnology* is applied to medical processes. Some examples are the designing of organisms to produce antibiotics, and the engineering of genetic cures through genomic manipulation. A rose plant that began as cells grown in a tissue culture
- *White biotechnology*, also known as industrial biotechnology, is biotechnology applied to industrial processes. An example is the designing of an organism to produce a useful chemical. Another example is the using of enzymes as industrial catalysts to either produce valuable chemicals or destroy hazardous/polluting chemicals. White biotechnology tends to consume less in resources than traditional processes used to produce industrial goods.
- *Blue biotechnology* is a term that has been used to describe the marine and aquatic applications of biotechnology, but its use is relatively rare. The investments and economic output of all of these types of applied biotechnologies form what has been described as the bioeconomy.
- Bioinformatics is an interdisciplinary field which addresses biological problems using computational techniques, and makes the rapid organization and analysis of biological data possible. The field may also be referred to as *computational biology*, and can be defined as, "conceptualizing biology in terms of molecules and then applying informatics techniques to understand and organize the information associated with these molecules, on a large scale." Bioinformatics plays a key role in various areas, such as functional genomics, tructural genomics, and proteomics, and forms a key component in the biotechnology and pharmaceutical sector.

Improve Yield from Crops

Using the techniques of modern biotechnology, one or two genes may be transferred to a highly developed crop variety to impart a new character that would increase its yield . However, YEA while increases in crop yield are the most obvious applications of modern biotechnology in agriculture, it is also the most difficult one. Current genetic engineering techniques work best for effects that are controlled by a single gene. Many of the genetic characteristics associated with yield (e.g., enhanced growth) are controlled by a large number of genes, each of which has a minimal effect on the overall yield. There is, therefore, much scientific work to be done in this area.

Reduced Vulnerability of Crops to Environmental Stresses

Crops containing genes that will enable them to withstand biotic and abiotic stresses may be developed. For example, drought and excessively salty soil are two important limiting factors in crop productivity. Biotechnologists are studying plants that can cope with these extreme conditions in the hope of finding the genes that enable them to do so and eventually transferring these genes to the more desirable crops. One of the latest developments is the identification of a plant gene, At-DBF2, from thale cress, a tiny weed that is often used for plant research because it is very easy to grow and its genetic code is well mapped out. When this gene was inserted into tomato and tobacco cells (see RNA interference), the cells were able to withstand environmental stresses like salt, drought, cold and heat, far more than ordinary cells. If these preliminary results prove successful in larger trials, then At-DBF2 genes can help in engineering crops that can better withstand harsh environments . Researchers have also created transgenic rice plants that are resistant to rice yellow mottle virus (RYMV). In Africa, this virus destroys majority of the rice crops and makes the surviving plants more susceptible to fungal infections .

Increased Nutritional Qualities of Food Crops

Proteins in foods may be modified to increase their nutritional qualities. Proteins in legumes and cereals may be transformed to provide the amino acids needed by human beings for a balanced diet. A good example is the work of Professors Ingo Potrykus and Peter Beyer on the so-called Goldenrice.

Improved Taste, Texture or Appearance of Food

Modern biotechnology can be used to slow down the process of spoilage so that fruit can ripen longer on the plant and then be transported to the consumer with a still reasonable shelf life. This improves the taste, texture and appearance of the fruit. More importantly, it could expand the market for farmers in developing countries due to the reduction in spoilage.

The first genetically modified food product was a tomato which was transformed to delay its ripening. Researchers in Indonesia, Malaysia, Thailand, Philippines and Vietnam are currently working on delayed-ripening papaya in collaboration with the University of Nottingham and Zeneca.

Biotechnology in Cheese Production

Enzymes produced by micro-organisms provide an alternative to animal rennet—a cheese coagulant—and an alternative supply for cheese makers. This also eliminates possible public concerns with animal-derived material, although there is currently no plans to develop synthetic milk, thus making this argument less compelling. Enzymes offer an animal-friendly alternative to animal rennet. While providing comparable quality, they are theoretically also less expensive.

About 85 million tons of wheat flour is used every year to bake bread. By adding an enzyme called maltogenic amylase to the flour, bread stays fresher longer. Assuming that 10-15% of bread is thrown away, if it could just stay fresh another 5–7 days then 2 million tons of flour per year would be saved. That corresponds to 40% of the bread consumed in a country such as the USA. This means more bread becomes available with no increase in input. In combination with other enzymes, bread can also be made bigger, more appetizing and better in a range of ways.

Reduced Dependence on Fertilizers, Pesticides and Other Agrochemicals

Most of the current commercial applications of modern biotechnology in agriculture are on reducing the dependence of farmers on agrochemicals. For example, *Bacillus thuringiensis* (*Bt*) is a soil bacterium that produces a protein with insecticidal qualities. Traditionally, a fermentation process has been used to produce an insecticidal spray from these bacteria. In this form, the Bt toxin occurs as an inactive protoxin, which requires digestion by an insect to be effective. There are several *Bt* toxins and each one is specific to certain target insects. Crop plants have now been engineered to contain and express the genes for Bt toxin, which they produce in its active form. When a susceptible insect ingests the transgenic crop cultivar expressing the Bt protein, it stops feeding and soon thereafter dies as a result of the Bt toxin binding to its gut wall. Bt corn is now commercially available in a number of countries to control corn borer (a lepidopteran insect), which is otherwise controlled by spraying (a more difficult process).

Crops have also been genetically engineered to acquire tolerance to broad-spectrum herbicide. The lack of cost-effective herbicides with broad-spectrum activity and no crop injury was a consistent limitation in crop weed management. Multiple applications of numerous herbicides were routinely used to control a wide range of weed species detrimental to agronomic crops. Weed management tended to rely on preemergence—that is, herbicide applications were sprayed in response to expected weed infestations rather than in response to actual weeds present. Mechanical cultivation and hand weeding were often necessary to control weeds not controlled by herbicide applications. The introduction of herbicide tolerant crops has the potential of reducing the number of herbicide active ingredients used for weed management, reducing the number of herbicide applications made during a season, and increasing yield due to improved weed management and less crop injury. Transgenic crops that express tolerance to glyphosate, glufosinate and bromoxynil have been developed. These herbicides can now be sprayed on transgenic crops without inflicting damage on the crops while killing nearby weeds. From 1996 to 2001, herbicide tolerance was the most dominant trait introduced to commercially available transgenic crops, followed by insect resistance. In 2001, herbicide tolerance deployed in soybean, corn and cotton accounted for 77% of the 626,000 square kilometres planted to transgenic crops; Bt crops accounted for 15%; and "stacked genes" for herbicide tolerance and insect resistance used in both cotton and corn accounted for 8 per cent.

Production of Novel Substances in Crop Plants

Biotechnology is being applied for novel uses other than food. For example, oilseed can be modified to produce fatty acids for detergents, substitute fuels and petrochemicals. Potatoes, tomatos, rice, tobacco, lettuce, safflowers, and other plants have been genetically-engineered to produce insulin and certain vaccines. If future clinical trials prove successful, the advantages of edible vaccines would be enormous, especially for developing countries. The transgenic plants may be grown locally and cheaply. Homegrown vaccines would also avoid logistical and economic problems posed by having to transport traditional preparations over long distances and keeping them cold while in transit. And since they are edible, they will not need syringes, which are not only an additional expense in the traditional vaccine preparations but also a source of infections if contaminated. In the case of insulin grown in transgenic plants, it is well-established that the gastrointestinal system breaks the protein down therefore this could not currently be administered as an edible protein. However, it might be produced at significantly lower cost than insulin produced in costly, bioreactors. For example, Calgary, Canada-based SemBioSys Genetics, Inc. reports that its safflower-produced insulin will reduce unit costs by over 25% or more and reduce the capital costs associated with building a commercial-scale insulin manufacturing facility by approximately over $100 million compared to traditional biomanufacturing facilities.

Biological engineering is a branch of engineering that focuses on biotechnologies and biological science. It includes different disciplines such as biochemical engineering, biomedical engineering, bio-process engineering, biosystem engineering and so on. Because of the novelty of the field, the definition of a bioengineer is still undefined. However, in general it is an integrated approach of fundamental biological sciences and Traditional engineering principles.

Bioengineers are often employed to scale up bio processes from the laboratory scale to the manufacturing scale. Moreover, as with most engineers, they often deal with management, economic and legal issues. Since patents and regulation (e.g. FDA regulation in the U.S.) are very important issues for biotech enterprises, bioengineers are often required to have knowledge related to these issues.

The increasing number of biotech enterprises is likely to create a need for bioengineers in the years to come. Many universities throughout the world are now providing programmes in bioengineering and biotechnology (as independent programs or specialty programs within more established engineering fields).

Microbiotechnology is being used to engineer and adapt organisms especially microorganisms in an effort to find sustainable ways to clean up contaminated environments. The elimination of a wide range of pollutants and wastes from the environment is an absolute requirement to promote a sustainable development of our society with low environmental impact. Biological processes play a major role in the removal of contaminants and biotechnology is taking advantage of the astonishing catabolic versatility of microorganisms to degrade/convert such compounds. New methodological breakthroughs in sequencing, genomics, proteomics, bioinformatics and imaging are producing vast amounts of information. In the field of Environmental Microbiology, genome-based global studies open a new era providing unprecedented *in silico* views of metabolic and regulatory networks, as well as clues to the evolution of degradation pathways and to the molecular adaptation strategies to changing environmental conditions. Functional genomic and metagenomic approaches are increasing our understanding of the relative importance of different pathways and regulatory networks to carbon flux in particular environments and for particular compounds and they will certainly accelerate the development of bioremediation technologies and biotransformation processes.

Marine environments are especially vulnerable since oil spills of coastal regions and the open sea are poorly containable and mitigation is difficult. In addition to pollution through human activities, millions of tons of petroleum enter the marine environment every year from natural seepages. Despite its toxicity, a considerable fraction of petroleum oil entering marine systems is eliminated by the hydrocarbon-degrading activities of microbial communities, in particular by a remarkable recently discovered group of specialists, the so-called hydrocarbonoclastic bacteria.

2

Insect Resistant Crops

INTRODUCTION

Agriculture in general leads to ecological disturbances as wild plant communities are replaced by monocultures of crop plants. In order to obtain sufficiently high yields, fertilisers are used and weeds combated by herbicides and tilling. Insect attack and fungal infections have to be minimised, both achieved conventionally by the application of pesticides which have adverse effects on the agricultural ecosystems. An alternative approach is to use genetically modified (GM) crops resistant to pests. It is just over ten years since the first GM crops were introduced yet they are very popular with farmers. In 2005 it was estimated that approved GM crops were grown globally on 90 million hectares, about 5% of all arable land; the increase between 2003 and 2005 alone was 33 per cent. Some 90% of those benefiting were resource-poor farmers from developing countries whose increased incomes from biotech crops contributed to the alleviation of their poverty. The Nuffield Council of Bioethics stated 1999 that "GM crops had a considerable potential to improve food security and the effectiveness for the agriculture in developing countries".

Whether the growth of GM crops is more economically rewarding and less damaging to the environment than the cultivation of their conventional counterparts with conventional protection by agrochemicals needs to be considered on a case-by-case basis. The present report deals with three important crops grown in developing countries: maize, rice and cotton, all with genetically engineered resistance towards feeding insects. This has been achieved by the expression within the crop plants of proteins (*Bt*-proteins) derived from the bacterium *Bacillus thuringensis*. Over 200 different *Bt*-proteins toxic to selected insects have been identified in various strains of this bacterium. For 40 years *Bt*-proteins have had a safe history as bio pesticides preparations and are approved for organic farming. Rats fed with very high doses of Bt-proteins showed no detectable toxic effects whereas synthetic pesticides, such as organophosphates and chlorinated biphenyls. are toxic. The high price of *Bt*-preparations, however, makes them expensive for use on commodity crops and they represent less than 2% of pesticides sold world-wide. Synthetic pesticides kill a very broad spectrum of insects, i.e. the target pests as well as beneficial insects, whereas *Bt*-crops kill primarily those insects attacking the crops.

Seeds incorporating *Bt* technology are particularly suitable for smallholder farmers, because they do not require the equipment and knowledge necessary for pesticide applications, and reduce farmers' exposure to insecticides, particularly for those using hand sprayers.

MAIZE

Worldwide, maize is the leading staple in tonnage terms. with two-thirds of the global hectarage grown in developing countries. It is noteworthy that the yields of maize harvested per hectare in the Corn Belt of the US can be 20 fold higher than that of resource-poor subsistence farmers in developing countries. Although most maize is used as animal feed, it is a staple food in many countries, particularly in Sub-Saharan Africa and South Asia. For example, the consumption of maize in Kenya has been reported to be 400g per person per day. In such countries it is imperative for food security that maize harvest yields are improved. Decreasing the harvest losses caused by insect pests is a major factor in yield improvement and stability.

On a global basis, the most important insect pests of maize are the larvae of various moths (corn borers). In temperate areas of America, and also more recently in Europe, rootworm larvae which damage roots have emerged as serious maize pests, with the yield losses in fields infested with rootworms as high as 50%. While rootworms can be combated by spraying organophosphates onto the soil, stem borers are difficult to control by pesticide spraying as the caterpillars penetrate into the plant. The application of pesticides has thus to target the caterpillars during the very short time between their emerging from the egg and entering the maize plant. *Bt*-maize, by contrast, has the advantage of the caterpillars being targeted when they feed on the plant and are so prevented from entering the stem. Although combating some pests will increase the population of others, the global deployment of Bt-genes to control maize pests has been estimated to have the potential of substituting 40-50% of the insecticides currently in use.

During the past ten years, hundreds of million people have consumed products from GM-maize and it has been widely used as animal feed. Yet, as discussed in an earlier report of our commission (Are there hazards for the consumer when eating food from genetically modified plants?), there is no evidence of the consumption of GM maize or its products being harmful to health. Moreover, there is clear evidence that GM maize offers the advantage of being much less subject to contamination by mycotoxins such as fumonisin and aflatoxin, toxins produced by fungi that infest maize cobs and which cause serious illnesses in man and animals. The invading fungi are opportunistic, primarily infecting kernels damaged by caterpillars; contamination by these powerful toxins can be so high that harvest products have to be withdrawn from the market. For subsistence farmers, e.g. in parts of Africa, the toxins cause grave health problems, particularly for children. The significantly lower mycotoxin contamination of GM maize is due to the fact that the cobs have fewer injuries. Thus, *Bt*-maize offers a critically important advantage for consumers concerned about food safety.

So far, maize *Bt* seeds have been distributed as hybrid varieties giving high yields, but the harvested grains cannot be used as farmer-saved seed. Critics of biotechnology often offer this as a reason why, in developing countries, Bt seeds are not suitable for smallholder farmers who mostly use farmer-saved seeds. However, hybrids are the predominant seed types in many developing countries. In China, the largest producer of maize after the USA, where maize is grown by 105 million farmers with an average holding of 0.23 hectare per farm, 84% have adopted hybrid seeds since they offer a higher return. For areas such as Central America and West Central Africa, where most of the maize is grown by subsistence farmers with farmer-saved seeds, nonprofit organisations are called upon to introduce Bt genes into local varieties so that these farmers may also profit from Bt technology.

Rice

World-wide, rice is the principal food for nearly two billion people, with the main producers being China, India and Indonesia. In these countries, rice is mostly grown by about 250 million smallholder farmers. Again, major insect pests are caterpillars such as stem borers and leaf-folders. At present, the productivity of rice plantations depends heavily on chemical inputs. The introduction of conventional pesticides about 30 years ago had a devastating impact on insect diversity, drastically reducing the populations of fish and crabs in the rice fields.

Many companies and institutions in the world, e.g. in Iran and Chi, are developing genetically modified insectresistant rice. Bt-ice cultivars have already been field-tested in Iran, China and Costa Rica, to be fully commercialized in due course. Field studies indicate that the introduction of Bt-rice has the potential for decreasing the amount of pesticides sprayed on the fields by more than 50% together with considerable increases in harvest yield.

Cotton

Cotton is grown in developing countries, mainly by smallholder farmers. The harvest is particularly threatened by insect pests such as the cotton bollworm, caterpillars, feeding within the fruit where the cotton fibres are produced. Without treatment, these pests can destroy most of the harvest.

Conventionally, they are combated by spraying organophosphate or pyrethroid pesticides. More pesticides are applied per hectare of cotton than to any other crop with the number of sprayings necessary per season varying from 2 to 12, but sometimes as high as 30.

Despite major expenditure of pesticides, cotton cultivation had totally collapsed in various regions of the world because of extremely high infestation levels.

For the past nine years, genetically modified cultivars containing a Bt-protein toxic to the cotton bollworm have been available. Their commercial introduction has been very successful: by 2005, Bt-cotton was grown on 28% of the global hectarage of cotton, with an increase of 33% in the last year. Whereas the Bt-cotton technology was originally commercialised by a single company in the US, it is now also distributed by a range of companies and institutions in China, India and elsewhere. In China in 2005 about 65% of the cotton was Btcultivars, and in South Africa as much as 85 per cent.

ECOLOGICALASPECTS

Experience with traditional crops shows that, through hybridisation, they can give rise to weeds requiring special cultural practices for their elimination. It is well established that gene flow occurs between both GM-cultivars and non-GM crops and their wild relatives. Cultivars of maize, rice and cotton sown as crops do not have sufficient biological fitness to survive in natural habitats; in most cases the incorporation of a few additional genes is unlikely to alter the fitness of a cultivar in a natural ecosystem. Maize has wild relatives only in Mexico and Central America whereas the wild relatives of cotton and rice are more widespread. So far, no transgenes have been observed to escape from maize or cotton to a wild relative, there permanently to initiate a selective advantage. In the wild, insect resistance could offer such a selective advantage but insect resistance mediated by a single gene is unlikely to persist. In the case of Bt-rice, particularly with modern rice cultivars designed for dry-land agriculture, special attention must be paid to the question of the possibility of gene flow to weedy wild rice relatives. It is surely relevant for such scenarios that, for more than 30 years, a very large number of rice cultivars have been grown into which single genes conferring resistance to certain insects had been introduced by conventional breeding. There are no known cases in which wild or weedy rice populations have become more competitive as a result of hybridisation with these cultivars.

Some years ago it was reported in a laboratory experiment that feeding Bt maize pollen caused considerable toxicity to Monarch butterflies and that survival of the species was threatened by this GM-crop. The report provoked so much public anxiety that the European Union passed a moratorium lasting several years on the approval of GM-crops. Extensive field studies, subsequently carried out by numerous investigators, clearly demonstrated that the cultivation of *Bt*-maize has no measurable impact on Monarch butterflies. A large number of studies with *Bt*-maize, rice and cotton, performed in several countries, have all shown that the populations of many non-target insects are higher in fields of *Bt*-cultivars than in fields of conventional crops regularly receiving applications of broad-spectrum pesticide.

There has been concern that Bt-proteins from the litter of plants and root exudates persist in the soil and have an impact on its fauna. Taking into account that agricultural soils are in any case highly modified by conventional cultivation, and particularly by tilling and the application of fertilisers and pesticides, the impact of *Bt*-crops on the fauna in the soil has been shown in extensive studies, including bioassays, to be irrelevant. As mentioned earlier, Bt-proteins are toxic only to selective insect pests. Combating those pests which are insensitive to the *Bt*-toxin means that in many cases the cultivation of Bt-cultivars still requires the application of pesticides although the number of pesticide sprays required is mostly much lower than with conventional cultivars. Decreases in pesticide applications are beneficial not only for the environment but also to farm labourers. Spraying chemical pesticides is a considerable health hazard, especially if hand sprayers are used. A survey in China revealed there were formerly on average 54 000 poisoning incidents annually, including 490 deaths due to the use of pesticides, and that the introduction of *Bt*-cotton cultivars reduced this health risk substantially. These facts provide overwhelming support for the beneficial effect of *Bt*-crops cultivation, both for the environment and for the health of the farm labourers. Economic aspects.

Since the seeds of *Bt*-cultivars are more expensive than their conventional alternatives, a farmer will have to decide whether infestation by pests is high enough to make the purchase GM seeds profitable. Although the returns for using Bt technology can result in reduced labour and pesticide costs, as well as increased harvest yields, there remain situations in which the expenditure for *Bt*-seeds does not pay off.

The fact that in 2003, 30% of maize and 46% of cotton in the US were planted as *Bt* cultivars clearly demonstrates that the Bt technology can indeed be profitable for farmers. The fact also that only 30% and 46% were planted suggests that there are circumstances in which the additional cost of the seeds is not justified. The decision of whether or not to use such seeds was made by individual American farmers on commercial grounds. This also applies to many developing countries. In China, where cotton is grown by about 11 million farmers with an average holding of 0.4 hectares, about 2/3 of these farmers have already adopted *Bt*-cotton. Bt technology is reported as being profitable because it leads in many cases both to a substantial decrease in pesticide use and to a yield increase.

In India, where cotton contributes 30% of the national agricultural gross domestic production and is grown mainly by smallholder farmers, the infestation of cotton fields by insect pests is very high and the average yield per area only about half of the world average. In India, only three years after the commercial release of *Bt* cotton, about 1 million farmers have decided to grow it. As reported, most, although not all of them, derived substantial profit as a result. Future success depends on the introduction of locally adapted varieties. In both China and India the distribution of *Bt* technology is no longer restricted to multinational companies but increasingly involves national companies and institutions, resulting in more competitive pricing.

The examples show clearly that Bt technology can indeed be valuable in economic terms to smallholder farmers with relatively small fields in developing countries as well as to the large farms in developed countries.

There is, however, the possibility that pests may become resistant to *Bt*-toxins as has happened in the past with the extensive use of organophosphates and pyrethroids. Although the evolution of resistant pests will not cause major ecological problems, it might gravely affect the economy of farmers and seed companies. In order to prevent such resistance, countries such as the US have adopted insect resistance management programs which include providing refuges of non-GM crops or other hosts. This ensures that susceptible insects are available in sufficient numbers to mate with any resistant survivors from Bt fields, so preventing the build-up of resistant insect populations. Thus far this system has worked well; almost all farmers obey the rules and several recent studies have failed to find resistance. Smallholder farmers do not have such problems, because they usually have several small fields with diverse crops.

World agriculture must continue to fulfil the food and fibre needs of the growing human population as well as rectify the existing widespread malnutrition. To achieve this aim, pest control will have to rely on integrated pest management practices which include crop rotation, biological control, Bt technology and the sparing use of pesticides. Bt technology has shown itself to be a valuable contribution to knowledgebased agriculture.

3

Cover Crop

Introduction

Broadly defined, a cover crop is any annual, biennial, or perennial plant grown as a monoculture (one crop type grown together) or polyculture (multiple crop types grown together), to improve any number of conditions associated with sustainable agriculture. Cover crops are fundamental, sustainable tools used to manage soil fertility, soil quality, water, weeds (unwanted plants that limit crop production potential), pests (unwanted animals, usually insects, that limit crop production potential), diseases, and diversity and wildlife, in agroecosystems. Agroecosystems are ecological systems managed by humans across a range of intensities to produce food, feed, or fiber. To a large degree, humans shape the ecological structure and function of natural processes that occur in agroecosystems. As agroecosystems often interact with neighboring natural ecosystems in agricultural landscapes, cover crops that improve the sustainability of agroecosystem attributes may also indirectly improve qualities of neighboring natural ecosystems. Farmers choose to grow specific cover crop types and to manage them in specific ways based on their own unique needs and goals. These needs and goals are influenced by biological, environmental, social, cultural, and economic factors of the food system within which farmers operate.

Soil Fertility Management

Cover crops also called "green manure" are used to manage a range of soil macronutrients and micronutrients. For example in Nigeria, the cover crop Mucuna pruriens (velvet bean) has been found to increase the availability of phosphorus in soil after a farmer applies rock phosphate. With respect to nutrients, the impact that cover crops have on nitrogen management has received by far the most attention by researchers and farmers, because nitrogen is often the most limiting nutrient in crop production. Cover crops known as "green manures" are grown and incorporated (by tillage) into the soil before reaching full maturity, and are intended to improve soil fertility and quality. They are commonly leguminous, meaning they are part of the fabaceae (pea) family. This family is unique in that all of the species in it set pods, such as bean, lentil, lupins and alfalfa. Leguminous cover crops are typically high in nitrogen and can often, to varying degrees, provide the required quantity of nitrogen for crop production that might normally be applied in chemical fertilizer form (called fertilizer replacement value). Another quality unique to leguminous cover crops is that they form symbiotic relationships with rhizobial bacteria that reside in legume root nodules. The genus Lupinus is nodulated by the soil microorganism Bradyrhizobium sp. (Lupinus). Bradyrhizobia are encountered as microsymbionts in other leguminous crops (Argyrolobium, Lotus, Ornithopus, Acacia, Lupinus) of Mediterranean origin. These bacteria convert biologically unavailable atmospheric nitrogen gas (N_2) to biologically available mineral nitrogen (NH_4^+) through the process of biological nitrogen fixation. Prior to the advent of the Haber-Bosch process, an energy-intensive method developed to carry out industrial nitrogen fixation and create chemical nitrogen fertilizer, most nitrogen introduced to ecosystems arose through biological nitrogen fixation. Some scientists believe that widespread biological nitrogen fixation, achieved mainly through the use of cover crops, is the only alternative to industrial nitrogen fixation in the effort to maintain or increase future food production levels . Industrial nitrogen fixation has been criticized as an unsustainable source of nitrogen for food production due to its reliance on fossil fuel energy and the environmental impacts associated with chemical nitrogen fertilizer use in agriculture. Such widespread environmental impacts include nitrogen fertilizer losses into waterways, which can lead to eutrophication (nutrient loading) and ensuing hypoxia (oxygen depletion) of large bodies of water. An example of this lies in the Mississippi Valley Basin, where years of fertilizer nitrogen loading into the watershed from agricultural production have resulted in a hypoxic "dead zone" off the Gulf of Mexico the size of New Jersey. The ecological complexity of marine life in this zone has been diminishing as a consequence. As well as bringing nitrogen into agroecosystems through biological nitrogen fixation, cover crops known as "catch crops" are used to retain and recycle soil nitrogen already present. The catch crops take up surplus nitrogen remaining from fertilization of the previous crop, preventing it from being lost through leaching or gaseous denitrification or volatilization. Catch crops are typically fast-growing annual cereal species adapted to scavenge available nitrogen efficiently from the soil. The nitrogen tied up in catch crop biomass is released back into the soil once the catch crop is incorporated as a green manure or otherwise begins to decompose.

Soil Quality Management

Cover crops can improve soil quality by increasing soil organic matter levels through the input of cover crop biomass over time. Increased soil organic matter enhances soil structure, as well as the water and nutrient holding and buffering capacity of soil). It can also lead to increased soil carbon sequestration, which has been promoted as a mitigation strategy to help offset the rise in atmospheric carbon dioxide levels.

Although cover crops can perform multiple functions in an agroecosystem simultaneously, they are often grown for the sole purpose of preventing soil erosion. Soil erosion is a process that can irreparably reduce the productive capacity of an agroecosystem. Dense cover crop stands physically slow down the velocity of rainfall before it contacts the soil surface, preventing soil splashing and erosive surface runoff

Additionally, vast cover crop root networks help anchor the soil in place and increase soil porosity, creating suitable habitat networks for soil macrofauna.

Soil quality is managed to produce optimum circumstances for crops to flourish. The principal factors of soil quality are soil salination, pH, microorganism balance and the prevention of soil contamination.

Water Management

By reducing soil erosion, cover crops often also reduce both the rate and quantity of water that drains off the field, that would normally pose environmental risks to waterways and ecosystems downstream. Cover crop biomass acts as a physical barrier between rainfall and the soil surface, allowing raindrops to steadily trickle down through the soil profile. Also, as stated above, cover crop root growth results in the formation of soil pores, which in addition to enhancing soil macrofauna habitat provides pathways for water to filter through the soil profile rather than draining off the field as surface flow. With increased water infiltration, the potential for soil water storage and the recharging of aquifers can be improved. Just before cover crops are killed (by such practices including mowing, tilling, discing, rolling, herbicide application) they contain a large amount of moisture. When the cover crop is incorporated into the soil, or left on the soil surface, it often increases soil moisture. In agroecosystems where water for crop production is in short supply, cover crops can be used as a mulch to conserve water by shading and cooling the soil surface. This reduces evaporation of soil moisture. In other situations farmers try to dry the soil out as quickly as possible going into the planting season. Here prolonged soil moisture conservation can be problematic. While cover crops can help to conserve water, in temperate regions (particularly in years with below average precipitation) they can draw down soil water supply in the spring, particularly if climatic growing conditions are good. In these cases, just before crop planting, farmers often face a tradeoff between the benefits of increased cover crop growth and the drawbacks of reduced soil moisture for cash crop production that season.

Weed Management

Thick cover crop stands often compete well with weeds during the cover crop growth period, and can prevent most germinated weed seeds from completing their life cycle and reproducing. If the cover crop is left on the soil surface rather than incorporated into the soil as a green manure after its growth is terminated, it can form a nearly impenetrable mat. This drastically reduces light transmittance to weed seeds, which in many cases reduces weed seed germination rates . Furthermore, even when weed seeds germinate, they often run out of stored energy for growth before building the necessary structural capacity to break through the cover crop mulch layer. This is often termed the *cover crop smother effect*. Some cover crops suppress weeds both during growth and after death. During growth these cover crops compete vigorously with weeds for available space, light, and nutrients, and after death they smother the next flush of weeds by forming a mulch layer on the soil surface. Researchers found that when using *Melilotus officinalis* (yellow sweetclover) as a cover crop in an improved fallow system (where a fallow period is intentionally improved by any number of different management practices, including the planting of cover crops), weed biomass only constituted between 1-12% of total standing biomass at the end of the cover crop growing season. Furthermore, after cover crop termination, the yellow sweetclover residues suppressed weeds to levels 75-97% lower than in fallow (no yellow sweetclover) systems In addition to competition-based or physical weed suppression, certain cover crops are known to suppress weeds through allelopathy. This occurs when certain biochemical cover crop compounds are degraded that happen to be toxic to, or inhibit seed germination of, other plant species. Some well known examples of allelopathic cover crops are *Secale cereale* (rye), *Vicia villosa* (hairy vetch), *Trifolium pretense* (red clover), *Sorghum bicolor* (sorghum-sudangrass), and species in the brassicaceae family, particularly mustards. In one study, rye cover crop residues were found to have provided between 80% and 95% control of early season broadleaf weeds when used as a mulch during the production of different cash crops such as soybean, tobacco, corn, and sunflower.

Disease Management

In the same way that allelopathic properties of cover crops can suppress weeds, they can also break disease cycles and reduce populations of bacterial and fungal diseases, and parasitic nematodes . Species in the brassicaceae family, such as mustards, have been widely shown to suppress fungal disease populations through the release of naturally occurring toxic chemicals during the degradation of glucosinolade compounds in their plant cell tissues.

Pest Management

Some cover crops are used as so-called "trap crops", to attract pests away from the crop of value and toward what the pest sees as a more favorable habitat. Trap crop areas can be established within crops, within farms, or within landscapes. In many cases the trap crop is grown during the same season as the food crop being produced. The limited area occupied by these trap crops can be treated with a pesticide once pests are drawn to the trap in large enough numbers to reduce the pest populations. In some organic systems, farmers drive over the trap crop with a large vacuum-based implement to physically pull the pests off the plants and out of the field. This system has been recommended for use to help control the pest lygus bug in organic strawberry production. Other cover crops are used to attract natural predators of pests by providing elements of their habitat. This is a form of biological control known as habitat augmentation, but achieved with the use of cover crops. Findings on the relationship between cover crop presence and predator/ pest population dynamics have been mixed, pointing toward the need for detailed information on specific cover crop types and management practices to best complement a given integrated pest management strategy. For example, the predator mite Euseius tularensis (Congdon) is known to help control the pest citrus thrips in Central California citrus orchards. Researchers found that the planting of several different leguminous cover crops (such as bell bean, woollypod vetch, New Zealand white clover, and Austrian winter pea) provided sufficient pollen as a feeding source to cause a seasonal increase in Congdon populations, which with good timing could potentially introduce enough predatory pressure to reduce pest populations of citrus thrips.

Diversity and Wildlife

Although cover crops are normally used to serve one of the above discussed purposes, they often simultaneously improve farm habitat for wildlife. The use of cover crops adds at least one more dimension of plant diversity to a cash crop rotation. Since the cover crop is typically not a crop of value, its management is usually less intensive, providing a window of "soft" human influence on the farm. This relatively "hands-off" management, combined with the increased on-farm heterogeneity created by the establishment of cover crops, increases the likelihood that a more complex trophic structure will develop to support a higher level of wildlife diversity). In one study, researchers compared arthropod and songbird species composition and field use between conventionally and cover cropped cotton fields in the Southern United States. The cover cropped cotton fields were planted to clover, which was left to grow in between cotton rows throughout the early cotton growing season (stripcover cropping). During the migration and breeding season, they found that songbird densities were 7–20 times higher in the cotton fields with integrated clover cover crop than in the conventional cotton fields. Arthropod abundance and biomass was also higher in the clover cover cropped fields throughout much of the songbird breeding season, which was attributed to an increased supply of flower nectar from the clover. The clover crop enhanced songbird habitat by providing cover and nesting sites, and an increased food source from higher arthropod populations.

4

Importance of Crop Rotation

Introduction

Satellite image of circular crop fields in Haskell County, Kansas in late June 2001. Healthy, growing crops are green. Corn would be growing into leafy stalks by then. Sorghum, which resembles corn, grows more slowly and would be much smaller and therefore, (possibly) paler. Wheat is a brilliant gold as harvest occurs in June. Fields of brown have been recently harvested and plowed under or lie fallow for the year.

Crop rotation or crop sequencing is the practice of growing a series of dissimilar types of crops in the same area in sequential seasons for various benefits such as to avoid the build up of pathogens and pests that often occurs when one species is continuously cropped. Crop rotation also seeks to balance the fertility demands of various crops to avoid excessive depletion of soil nutrients. A traditional component of crop rotation is the replenishment of nitrogen through the use of green manure in sequence with cereals and other crops. It is one component of polyculture. Crop rotation can also improve soil structure and fertility by alternating deep-rooted and shallow-rooted plants.

Method and Purpose

Crop rotation avoids a decrease in soil fertility, as growing the same crop repeatedly in the same place eventually depletes the soil of various nutrients. A crop that leaches the soil of one kind of nutrient is followed during the next growing season by a dissimilar crop that returns that nutrient to the soil or draws a different ratio of nutrients, for example, rices followed by cottons. By crop rotation farmers can keep their fields under continuous production, without the need to let them lie fallow, and reducing the need for artificial fertilizers, both of which can be expensive. Rotating crops add nutrients to the soils.

Legumes, plants of the family Fabaceae, for instance, have nodules on their roots which contain nitrogen-fixing bacteria. It therefore makes good sense agriculturally to alternate them with cereals (family Poaceae) and other plants that require nitrates. A common modern crop rotation is alternating soybeans and maize (corn). In subsistence farming, it also makes good nutritional sense to grow beans and grain at the same time in different fields.

Crop rotation is also used to control pests and diseases that can become established in the soil over time. Plants within the same taxonomic family tend to have similar pests and pathogens. By regularly changing the planting location, the pest cycles can be broken or limited. For example, root-knot nematode is a serious problem for some plants in warm climates and sandy soils, where it slowly builds up to high levels in the soil, and can severely damage plant productivity by cutting off circulation from the plant roots. Growing a crop that is not a host for root-knot nematode for one season greatly reduces the level of the nematode in the soil, thus making it possible to grow a susceptible crop the following season without needing soil fumigation.

It is also difficult to control weeds similar to the crop which may contaminate the final produce. For instance, ergot in weed grasses is difficult to separate from harvested grain. A different crop allows the weeds to be eliminated, breaking the ergot cycle.

The choice and sequence of rotation crops depends on the nature of the soil, the climate, and precipitation which together determine the type of plants that may be cultivated. Other important aspects of farming such as crop marketing and economic variables must also be considered when choosing a crop rotation.

Early Crop Rotation Methods

Early crop rotation methods were mentioned in Roman literature, and referred to by several civilizations in Asia and Africa. During the Muslim Agricultural Revolution of the Islamic Golden Age, Muslim engineers and farmers introduced a new modern rotation system where land was cropped four times or more in a two-year period. Winter crops were followed by summer ones, and in some cases there was a crop in between. In areas where plants of shorter growing season were used, ie.spinach and eggplants, the land could be cropped three or more times a year. According to some sources, in parts of Yemen wheat yielded two harvests a year on the same land, as did rice in Iraq. Scholars such as Andrew Watson have written of a Muslim agricultural revolution as the Islamic world made significant progress in developing a more "scientific" approach based on three major elements: sophisticated systems of crop rotation, highly developed irrigation techniques and introduction of a large variety of crops which were studied and catalogued according to the season, type of land and amount of water they require. Numerous farming encyclopaedias, with surprisingly great precision and details, were produced.

From the end of the Middle Ages until the 20th century, the three-year rotation was practiced by farmers in Europe with a rotation of rye or winter wheat, followed by spring oats or barley, then letting the soil rest (leaving it fallow) during the third stage. The fact that suitable rotations made it possible to restore or to maintain a productive soil has long been recognized by planting spring crops for livestock in place of grains for human consumption.

A four-field rotation was pioneered by farmers, namely in the region Waasland in the early 16th century and popularised by the British agriculturist Charles Townshend in the 18th century. The system (wheat, barley, turnips and clover), opened up a fodder crop and grazing crop allowing livestock to be bred year-round. The four-field crop rotation was a key development in the British Agricultural Revolution.

George Washington Carver pioneered crop rotation methods in the United States by teaching southern farmers to rotate soil depleting crops like cotton with soil enriching crops like peanuts and peas.

In the Green revolution, the traditional practice of crop rotation gave way in some parts of the world to the practice of supplementing the chemical inputs to the soil through top dressing with fertilizers, e.g., adding ammonium nitrate or urea and restoring soil pH with lime in the search for increased yields, preparing soil for specialist crops, and seeking to reduce waste and inefficiency by simplifying planting and harvesting. Some disadvantages of this type of monoculture have since become apparent, notably from the perspective of sustainable agriculture and the risk of catastrophic crop failure.

5

Agricultural Ecosystems

INTRODUCTION

Managing genetic resources on farms concerns the entire ecosystem, including cultivated crops, forages and agroforestry species, as well as their wild and weedy relatives that may be rowing in near by area.

There are many benefits from effective on farm genetic resources managementprogrammeso find out more, keep scrolling down or click on the links below:

- Conserving the processes of evolution and adaptation Conserving and using diversity at different levels.
- Integrating farmers into a national plant genetic resources system.
- Improving the livelihoods of resource-poor farmers.
- Maintaining or increasing farmers control and access over genetic resources Managing stress and change.
- Seed systems and diversity maintenance
- Ecosystem services linking wild and cultivated systems

Conserving the Processes of Evolution and Adaptation

The conservation and use of agrobiodiversity at all levels within local environments helps ensure that the ongoing processes of evolution and adaptation of crops to their environments are maintained within farming systems. This benefit is central to *in situ* management of genetic resources, as it is based on conserving and using not only existing germplasm but also the conditions that allow for the development of new germplasm.

Conserving and using Diversity at Different Levels

In its maintenance of farming systems, on-farm conservation applies the principle of conservation and use to all three levels of biodiversity: ecosystem, species and genetic (intraspecific) diversity. In conserving the structure of the agroecosystem, with its different niches and the interactions among them, the evolutionary processes and environmental pressures that affect genetic diversity are maintained and this contributes to the overall health of the local environment.

Integrating Farmers into a National Plant Genetic Resources System

Farmers are likely to know the nature and extent of local crop resources better than anyone through their daily interactions with the diversity in their fields. Given their expertise, incorporation of farmers into the national genetic resources system can help create productive partnerships for all involved. This integration can happen in several ways, including:

- Seeing farmers as partners in the maintenance of selected germplasm.
- Establishing a national dialogue on biodiversity conservation, sustainable use and equitable benefit-sharing between farmers, genebanks and other partners.
- Assisting the exchange of information with and among farmers from different sites and projects.
- Farmers visiting genebanks or seeing demonstrations by genebanks.
- Developing systems to make genebank material more easily accessible to farmers.

Improving the Livelihoods of Resource-poor Farmers

In situ on farm genetic resource management programmes also have significant potential to improve the livelihoods of farmers at the local level. On-farm conservation and use programmes can be combined with local infrastructure development or the increased access for farmers to useful germplasm held in national genebanks.

Farmers benefit from the continued agricultural diversity and ecosystem health that these programmes support. Local crop resources can be the basis for initiatives to increase crop production or secure new marketing opportunities. By building development efforts on local resources and through the empowerment of farming communities, they can lead to sustainable livelihood improvement. Resource-poor farmers, in particular, may benefit if development initiatives are not based on external inputs that may be costly or inappropriate for marginal agroecosystems.

Maintaining or Increasing Farmers Control and Access Over Genetic Resources

On-farm conservation and use also serves to empower farmers to control the genetic resources in their fields. On-farm genetic resource management recognizes farmers and communities as the curators of local biodiversity and the traditional knowledge to which it is linked. In turn, farmers are more likely to reap any benefits that arise from the genetic material they are managing.

Managing Stress and Change

Managing agroecosytems and the biodiversity they contain is essential for human health and nutrition and for the continued availability of food and other agricultural products.

Crop diversity can be used as a resource to mediate potential stresses of the surrounding environment. A crop population with a diverse genetic makeup may have a lower risk of being entirely lost to any particular stress, such as temperature extremes, droughts, floods, pests, and other environmental variables. Crops with different planting times and times to maturity give the farmer the option to plant and harvest crops at multiple points in the season to guard against total crop loss to environmental threats.

Farmers shape the degree and distribution of genetic diversity in their crops both directly, through selection, and indirectly, through management of different agroecosystem components. For many farmers in developing countries, the availability of adaptive varieties for particular micro-niches may be one of the few resources available to increase or maintain production on his or her field.

Seed Systems and Diversity Maintenance

Each year farmers decide how much seed to plant and where that seed comes from. These seeds may come through formal and informal systems, and may contain new combinations of genes that result from hybridization and introgression between wild and cultivated plants or among cultivated varieties.

Whether new combinations of genes or new seed types are maintained, with the resultant development of populations with new characteristics depends on farmer management and access. Rather than being passive recipients of seed from the formal sector (government, extension agencies, seed companies), farmers participate in dynamic networks of seed exchange and development.

On farm biodiversity management programmes that support strong seed supply systems can foster increased use of diversity while fulfilling certain types of farmer seed demand. Strong seed supply systems enable farmers to maintain a high level of diversity over time, despite losses of seed stock, bottlenecks, and other regular or unanticipated losses of crops genetic diversity.

Research on seed systems has shown that:

- a very large percentage of the seeds used by farmers in developing countries is acquired by informal means such as local markets, friends and relatives;

- farmers engage in the innovation of new varieties by actively seeking our new seed or saving seed of plants that display new traits in their fields;
- farmers retain diversity according to environmental conditions, market demands, culinary and aesthetic preferences, and social factors like religion and prestige farmers blend modern and traditional varieties.

Seed systems may shape crop genetic diversity and that seed systems can act as linkages between very distinct populations.

Ecosystem Services

One commonly cited justification for maintaining plant genetic diversity in agricultural production systems generally, and in farmers' fields in particular, is its ability to buffer or limit disease and pest epidemics. When many farmers sow varieties that carry the same genetic mechanism of resistance to a plant disease, the crop is vulnerable to epidemics. The complexity of crop-pest interactions in agroecosystems is compounded by their seasonal or annual variability, particularly in stressful environments of extreme temperature sand unpredictable rainfall.

Combating epidemics once they occur can be costly to society both in terms of garnering the resources necessary to control them and the yield losses incurred, and especially so in developing countries.

By conserving and harnessing ecosystem biodiversity, on farm genetic resource management programmes can provide other valuable services to farmers. For example, the value of having a diversity of pollinators, such as bees, butterflies, hummingbirds and even bats is immense. Plus, soil biodiversity helps keep farmers' field fertile.

Linking Wild and Cultivated Systems

On farm biodiversity management programmes can serve to increase out knowledge about the links between wild crop species andcultivateones ther new combinations of genes that result from hybridization and introgression between wild and cultivated crops are maintained, with the resultant development of populations with new characteristics, depends on natural selection, and in of crops, on human selection.

While many cases of deliberate introgression of desirable traits into crop cultivars as part of breeding programs are known, the extent and significance of natural or farmer assisted introgression is uncertain. A range techniques has been used to document natural hybridization and introgression of agricultural crops and their wild relatives in many crops including maize, wheat, barley, oats, pearl millet, foxtail millet, quinoa, hops, hemp, potato, casava, common bean, cowpea, pigeon pea, carrots, squash,tomato, radish, lettuce, chili, beets, sunflower, cabbage, and raspberries. However, the majority of these studies are based on morphological characters, and few have investigated the frequency with which such new types are produced and retained in natural and agro ecosystems for farmer selection.

Even more limited is information on the role of farmers in recognizing and selecting new genetic variation from the natural introgression of crops with their wild relatives, and the impact, once selected, of these new genetic combinations on the crop diversity.

6

Plant Diseases

Introduction

Plant pathology (also called phytopathology) is the scientific study of plant diseases caused by pathogens (infectious diseases) and environmental conditions (physiological factors). Organisms that cause infectious disease include fungi, oomycetes, bacteria, viruses, viroids, virus-like organisms, phytoplasmas, protozoa, nematodes and parasitic plants. Not included are insects, mites, vertebrate or other pests that affect plant health by consumption of plant tissues. Plant pathology also involves the study of the identification, etiology, disease cycle, economic impact, epidemiology, how plant diseases affect humans and animals, pathosystem genetics and management of plant diseases.

Plant Pathogens

The *"Disease triangle"* is a central concept of plant pathology for infectious disease . It is based on the principle that disease is the result of an interaction between a host, a pathogen, and environment condition.

Fungi

The fungi reproduce both sexually and asexually via the production of spores. These spores may be spread long distances by air or water, or they may be soil bourne. Many soil bourne spores, normally zoospores and capable of living saprotrophically, carrying out the first part of their lifecycle in the soil. Fungal diseases can be controlled through the use of fungicides in agriculture, however new races of fungi often evolve that are resistant to various fungicides.

Significant fungal plant pathogens are as follows:

Ascomycetes

- *Fusarium* spp.
- *Thielaviopsis* spp. (Causal agents of: canker rot, black root rot, *Thielaviopsis* root rot)
- *Verticillium* spp.
- *Magnaporthe grisea* (T.T. Hebert) M.E. Barr; causes blast of rice and gray leaf spot in turfgrasses

Basidiomycetes

- *Rhizoctonia* spp.
- *Phakospora pachyrhizi* Sydow; causes Soybean rust
- *Puccinia* spp.; causal agents of severe rusts of virtually all cereal grains and cultivated grasses

Oomycetes

The oomycetes are fungal-like organisms that until recently used to be mistaken for fungi. They include some of the most destructive plant pathogens including the genus *Phytophthora* which includes the casual agents of potato late blight and sudden oak death.

Despite not being closely related to the fungi, the oomycetes have developed very similar infection strategies and so many plant pathologists group them with fungal pathogens.

Significant oomycete plant pathogens

- *Pythium* spp.
- *Phytophthora* spp.; including the causal agent of the Great Irish Famine (1845-1849)
- Rice blast is hemibiotrophic

Bacteria

Crown gall disease caused by Agrobacterium Most bacteria that are associated with plants are actually saprotrophic, and do no harm to the plant itself. However, a small number, around 100 species, are able to cause disease. Bacterial diseases are much more prevalent in sub-tropical and tropical regions of the world.

Most plant pathogenic bacteria are rod shaped (bacilli). In order to be able to colonise the plant they have specific pathogenicity factors. There are four main bacterial pathogenicity factors:

1. *Cell wall degrading enzymes:* used to break down the plant cell wall in order to release the nutrients inside. Used by pathogens such as Erwinia to cause soft rot.
2. *Toxins* These can be non-host specific, and damage all plants, or host specific and only cause damage on a host plant.
3. *Phytohormones:* for example Agrobacterium changes the level of Auxin to cause tumours.
4. *Exopolysaccharides:* these are produced by bacteria and block xylem vessels, often leading to the death of the plant.

Bacteria control the production of pathogenicity factors via quorum sensing.

Significant bacterial plant pathogens:

- Burkholderia
- Proteobacteria
- *Xanthomonas* spp.
- *Pseudomonas* spp.

Phytoplasmas ('Mycoplasma-like organisms') and spiroplasmas

Phytoplasma and *Spiroplasma* are a genre of bacteria that lack cell walls, and are related to the mycoplasmas which are human pathogens. Together they are referred to as the mollicutes. They also tend to have smaller genomes than true bacteria. They are normally transmitted by sap-sucking insects, being transferred into the plants phloem where it reproduces.

Viruses, Viroids and Virus-like Organisms

There are many types of plant virus, and some are even asymptomatic. Normally plant viruses only cause a loss of yield. Therefore it is not economically viable to try to control them, the exception being when they infect perennial species, such as fruit trees. Most plant viruses have small, single stranded RNA genomes. These genomes may only encode 3 or 4 proteins: a replicase, a coat protein, a movement protein to allow cell to cell movement and sometimes a protein that allows transmission by a vector. Plant viruses must be transmitted from plant to plant by a vector. This is normally an insect, but some fungi, nematodes and protozoa have been shown to be viral vectors.

Nematodes

Nematodes are small, multicelluar wormlike creatures. Many live freely in the soil, but there are some species which parasitize plant roots. They are mostly a problem in tropical and subtropical regions of the world, where they may infect crops. Root-knot nematodes have quite a large host range, whereas cyst nematodes tend to only be able to infect a few species. Nematodes are able to cause radical changes in root cells in order to facilitate their lifestyle.

Protozoa

There are a few examples of plant diseases caused by protozoa. They are transmitted as zoospores which are very durable, and may be able to survive in a resting state in the soil for many years. They have also been shown to transmit plant viruses. When the motile zoospores come into contact with a root hair they produce a plasmodium and invade the roots.

Parasitic Plants

Parasitic plants such as mistletoe and dodder are included in the study of phytopathology. Dodder, for example, is used as a conduit for the transmission of virues or virus-like agents from a host plant to either a plant that is not typically a host or for an agent that is not graft-transmissible.

Plant Disease Forecasting

Plant disease forecasting is a management system used to predict the occurrence or change in severity of plant diseases. At the field scale, these systems are used by growers to make economic decisions about disease treatments for control. Often the systems ask the grower a series of questions about the susceptibility of the host crop, and incorporate current and forecast weather conditions to make a recommendation. Typically a recommendation is made about whether disease treatment is necessary or not. Usually treatment is a pesticide application. Forecasting systems are based on assumptions about the pathogen's interactions with the host and environment, the disease triangle. The objective is to accurately predict when the three factors - host, environment, and pathogen - all interact in such a fashion that disease can occur and cause economic losses.

In most cases the host can be suitably defined as resistant or susceptible, and the presence of the pathogen may often be reasonably ascertained based on previous cropping history or perhaps survey data. The environment is usually the factor that controls whether disease develops or not. Environmental conditions may determine the presence of the pathogen in a particular season through their effects on processes such as overwintering. Environmental conditions also affect the ability of the pathogen to cause disease, e.g. a minimum leaf wetness duration is required for grey leaf spot of corn to occur. In these cases a disease forecasting system attempts to define when the environment will be conducive to disease development. Good disease forecasting systems must be reliable, simple, cost-effective and applicable to many diseases. As such they are normally only designed for diseases that are irregular enough to warrant a prediction system, rather than diseases that occur every year for which regular treatment should be employed. Forecasting systems can only be designed if there is also an understanding on the actual disease triangle parameters.

Examples of Disease Forecasting Systems

Forecasting systems may use one of several parameters in order to work out disease risk, or a combination of factors One of the first forecasting systems designed was for Stewart's Wilt and based on winter temperature index as low temperatures would kill the vector of the disease so there would be no outbreak. An example of a multiple disease/pest forecasting system is the EPIdemiology, PREdiction, and PREvention (EPIPRE) System developed in the Netherlands for winter wheat that focused on multiple pathogens. Forecasting models are often based on a relationship like simple linear regression where x is used to predict y. Other relationships can be modelled using population growth curves. The growth curve that is used will depend on the nature of the epidemic. Polycyclic epidemics such as potato late blight are usually best modelled by using the logistic model, whereas monocyclic epidemics may be best modelled using the monomolecular model. Correct choice of a model is essential for a disease forecasting system to be useful.

Plant disease forecasting models must be thoroughly tested and validated after being developed. Interest has arisen lately in model validation through the quantification of the economic costs of false positives and false negatives, where disease prevention measures may be used when unnecessary or not applied when needed respectively The costs of these two types of errors need to be weighed carefully before deciding to use a disease forecasting system.

Future Developments

In the future, disease forecasting systems may become more useful as computing power increases and the amount of data that is available to plant pathologists to construct models increases. Good forecasting systems also may become increasingly important with climate change. It will be important to be able to accurately predict where disease outbreaks may occur, since they may not be in the historically known areas.

Plant Virus

Plant viruses, like all other viruses, are obligate intracellular parasites that do not have the molecular machinery to replicate without the host. The plant viruses are defined as viruses pathogenic to higher plants. While this article does not intend to list all plant viruses, it discusses some important viruses as well as their uses in plant molecular biology.

Overview

Although plant viruses are not nearly as well understood as the animal counterparts, one plant virus has become iconic. The first virus to be discovered (see below) was *Tobacco mosaic virus* (TMV). This and other viruses cause have an estimated US$60 billion per year economic influence on crops worldwide. Plant viruses are grouped into 73 genera and 49 families.

History

The discovery of plant viruses causing disease is often accredited to Martinus Beijerinck who determined, in 1898, that plant sap obtained from tobacco leaves with the "mosaic disease" remained infectious when passed through a porcelain filter. This was in contrast to bacteria microorganisms, which were retained by the filter. Beijerinck referred to the infectious filtrate as a "contagium vivum fluidum", thus the coinage of the modern term "virus". After the initial discovery of the 'viral concept' there was need to classify any other known viral diseases based on the mode of transmission even though microscopic observation proved fruitless. In 1939 Holmes published a classification list of 129 plant viruses. This was expanded and in 1999 there were 977 officially recognized, and some provisional, plant virus species.

The purification (crystallization) of the TMV was first performed by Wendell Stanley, who published his findings in 1935, although he did not determine that the RNA was the infectious material. However, he received the Nobel Prize in Chemistry in 1946. In the 1950s a discovery by two labs simultaneously proved that the purified RNA of the TMV was infectious which reinforced the argument. The RNA was carrying genetic information to code for the production of new infectious particles. More recently virus research has been focused on understanding the genetics and molecular biology of plant virus genomes, with a particular interest in determining how the virus can replicate, move, and infect plants. Understanding the virus genetics and protein functions has been used to explore the potential for commercial use by biotechnology companies. In particular, viral-derived sequences have been used to provide an understanding of novel forms of resistance. The recent boom in technology allowing humans to manipulate plant viruses may provide new strategies for production of value-added proteins in plants.

Structure

Viruses are very small and can only be observed with an electron microscope. The structure of a virus is given by its coat of proteins, which surround the viral genome. Assembly of viral particles takes place spontaneously. Over 50% of known plant viruses are rod shaped (flexuous or rigid). The length of the particle is normally dependent on the genome but it is usually between 300–500 nm with a diameter of 15–20 nm. Protein subunits can be placed around the circumference of a circle to form a disc. In the presence of the viral genome, the discs are stacked, then a tube is created with room for the nucleic acid genome in the middle.

The second most common structure amongst plant viruses are isometric particles. They are 40–50 nm in diameter. In cases when there is only a single coat protein, the basic structure consists of 60 T subunits, where T is an integer. Some viruses may have 2 coat proteins are the formation of the particle is analogous to a football.

There are three genera of *Geminiviridae* that possess geminate particles which are like two isometric particles stuck together. A very small number of plant viruses have, in addition to their coat proteins, a lipid envelope. This is derived from the plant cell membrane as the virus particle buds off from the cell.

Transmission of Plant Viruses through Sap

It implies direct transfer of sap by contact of and wounded plant with a healthy one. Such process occurs during agricultural practices by tools, hands, or by animal feeding on the plant. Generally TMV, potato viruses and cucumber mosaic viruses are transmitted via sap.

Insects

Plant viruses need to be transmitted by a vector, most often insects such as leafhoppers. One class of viruses, the Rhabdoviridae, have been proposed to actually be insect viruses that have evolved to replicate in plants. The chosen insect vector of a plant virus will often be the determining factor in that virus' host range: it can only infect plants that the insect vector feeds upon. This was shown in part when the old world white fly made it to the USA, where it transferred many plant viruses onto new hosts.

Depending on the way they are transmitted, plant viruses are classified as non-persistent, semi-persistent and persistent. In non-persistent transmission, viruses become attached to the distal tip of the stylet of the insect and on the next plant it feeds on, it inoculates it with the virus. Semi-persistent viral transmission involves the virus entering the foregut of the insect. Those viruses that manage to pass through the gut into the haemolymph and then to the salivary glands are known as persistent.

There are two sub-classes of persistent viruses: propergative and circulative. Propergative viruses are able to replicate in both the plant and the insect (and may have originally been insect viruses), whereas circulative can not. Many plant viruses encode within their genome polypeptides with domains essential for transmission by insects. In non-persistent and semi-persistent viruses, these domains are in the coat protein and another protein known as the helper component. A bridging hypothesis has been proposed to explain how these proteins aid in insect-mediated viral transmission. The helper component will bind to the specific domain of the coat protein, and then the insect mouthparts—creating a bridge. In persistent propagative viruses, such as tomato spotted wilt virus (TSWV), there is often a lipid coat surrounding the proteins that is not seen in the other classes of plant viruses. In the case of TSWV, 2 viral proteins are expressed in this lipid envelope. It has been proposed that the viruses bind via these proteins and are then taken into the insect cell by receptor-mediated endocytosis.

Nematodes

Soil-borne nematodes also have been shown to transmit viruses. They acquire and transmit them by feeding on infected roots. Viruses can be transmitted by non-persistently and persistently, but there is no evidence of viruses being able to replicate in nematodes.

Plasmodiophorids

A number of viral genera are transmitted, both persistently and non-persistently, by soil borne zoosporic protozoa. These protozoa are not phytopathogenic themselves, but parasitic. Transmission of the virus takes place when they become associated with the plant roots. An example is *Polymyxa graminis,* which has been shown to transmit a plant viral diseases in ceral crops

Seed and Pollen Borne Viruses

Plant virus transmission from generation to generation occurs in about 20% of plant viruses. When viruses are transmitted by seeds, the seed is infected in the generative cells and the virus is maintained in the germ cells and sometimes, but less often, in the seed coat. When the growth and development of plants is delayed because of situations like unfavourable weather, there is an increase in the amount of virus infections in seeds. There does not seem to be a correlation between the location of the seed on the plant and its chances of being infected. Little is known about the mechanisms involved in the transmission of plant viruses via seeds, although it is known that it is environmentally influenced and that seed transmission occurs because of a direct invasion of the embryo via the ovule or by an indirect route with an attack on the embryo mediated by infected gametes. These processes can occur concurrently or separately depending on the host plant. It is unknown how the virus is able to directly invade and cross the embryo and boundary between the parental and progeny generations in the ovule. Many plants species can be infected through seeds including but not limited to the families Leguminoseae, Solanacease, Compositae, Rosaceae, Curcurbitaceae, Gramineae.

Translation of Plant Viral Proteins

As mentioned above, 90% of plant viruses have genomes that consist of single stranded RNA, meaning that they are in the same sense orientation as messenger RNA. Viruses use the plant ribosomes to produce the 4-10 proteins encoded by their genome. However, since all of the proteins are encoded on a single strand (that is, they are polycistronic) this will mean that the ribosome will either only produce one protein, as it will terminate translation at the first stop codon or that a polyprotein will be produced. Plant viruses have had to evolve special techniques to allow the production of viral proteins by plant cells. In order for translation to occur eukaryotic mRNAs require a 5' Cap structure. This means that viruses must also have one. This normally consists of 7MeGpppN where N is normally adenine or guanine. The viruses encode a protein, normally a replicase, with a methyltransferase activity to allow this.

Some viruses are cap-snatchers. During this process, a 7mG-capped host mRNA is recruited by the viral transcriptase complex and subsequently cleaved by a virally encoded endonuclease. The resulting capped leader RNA is used to prime transcription on the viral genome. However some plant viruses do not use cap, yet translate efficiently due to cap-independent translation enhancers present in 5' and 3' untranslated regions of viral mRNA.

Production of Sub-genomic RNAs

Some viruses use the production of sub-genomic RNAs to ensure the translation of all proteins within their genomes. In this process the first protein encoded on the genome, and this the first to be translated, is a replicase. This protein will act of the rest of the genome producing negative strand sub-genomic RNAs then act upon these to form positive strand sub-genomic RNAs that are essentially mRNAs ready for translation.

Segmented Genomes

Some viral families, such as the *Bromoviridae* instead opt to have multi-partite genomes, genomes split between multiple viral particles. For infection to occur, the plant must be infected with all particles across the genome. For instance *Brome mosaic virus* has a genome split between 3 viral particles, and all three particles with the different RNAs are required for infection to take place.

Global Plant Clinic

The Global Plant Clinic (GPC) is managed by CABI in alliance with Rothamsted Research and the Central Science Laboratory. The GPC provides plant health services and supports over 80 plant health clinics in Africa, Asia and Latin America. The clinic has a diagnostic service, which covers all plants and types of problems, is used by over 80 countries and helps maintain disease vigilance. The clinic also trains plant pathologists, and work with all sectors to improve regular and reliable access to technical support and advice. The clinics main aim is to create durable plant health services for those who need them most by improving access to technical support and advice.

Origins

Identifying plant pathogens was one of the original aims of the Imperial Bureau of Mycology which eventually became part of the Commonwealth Agricultural Bureaux (CAB) that included scientists with special skills in mycology, entomology, nematodes and later bacteria. The Commonwealth Agricultural Bureaux was later renamed CABI in 1992. CABI works predominantly in and with developing countries. In the 1980s, the then Overseas Development Administration (now the Department for International Development) began funding a diagnostic and advisory service for plant diseases. Jim Waller, Ian Gibson, Dick Pawsey and others became plant pathology 'liaison officers', investigating major problems such as Sumatra Disease of Cloves in Indonesia and providing technical support to many plant pathology disease projects that were funded by the UK government.

When DFID was created by the Labour Government in 1997 this also signalled a major change in development policies. The diagnostic and advisory service changed its name in 2002 to the Global Plant Clinic and itself undertook a major change in terms of priorities and activities . The core diagnostic services for fungal, bacterial and nematode diseases were maintained and widened to include viruses and phytoplasmas. Phil Jones, based at Rothamsted Research, had been jointly funded with IMI to provide such services from the 1990s but it was not until 2005 that Rothamsted Research and the Central Science Laboratory were both formally incorporated in the GPC alliance.

Plant Health Services

The GPC created several plant health clinics that could be run independently by organisations in-country. The first country to try these out was Bolivia, pioneered by CIAT Bolivia and Proinpa, soon followed by Uganda and then Bangladesh. The early experiences led to interest from Nicaragua, which now has the largest and most extensive network of clinics (called Puestos para Plantas) linked to a revitalised network for diagnostics and plant health management Other countries which have adopted plant health clinics include Sierra Leone, Democratic Republic of the Congo, Rwanda, India and Vietnam. The GPC has carried out pilot clinics in Peru and Indonesia.

PHYTOPLASMA

Phytoplasma

A palm tree dying of lethal yellowing phytoplasma.

Scientific Classification

Division : irmicutes

Class : Mollicutes

Order : Acholeplasmatales

Family : Acholeplasmataceae

Genus : ***Candidatus* Phytoplasma**

Species

"*Ca.* Phytoplasma *allocasuarinae*"

"*Ca.* Phytoplasma *asteris*"

"*Ca.* Phytoplasma *aurantifolia*"

"*Ca.* Phytoplasma *australiense*"

"*Ca.* Phytoplasma *brasiliense*"

"*Ca.* Phytoplasma *castaneae*"

"*Ca.* Phytoplasma *cocostanzaniae*"

"*Ca.* Phytoplasma *cocosnigeriae*"

"*Ca.* Phytoplasma *cynodontis*"

"*Ca.* Phytoplasma *fraxini*"

"*Ca.* Phytoplasma *japonicum*"

"*Ca.* Phytoplasma *luffae*"

"*Ca.* Phytoplasma *mali*"

"*Ca.* Phytoplasma *oryzae*"

"*Ca.* Phytoplasma *palmae*"

"*Ca.* Phytoplasma *phoenicium*"

"*Ca.* Phytoplasma *pruni*"

"*Ca.* Phytoplasma *prunorum*"

"*Ca.* Phytoplasma *pyri*"

"*Ca.* Phytoplasma *rhamni*"

"*Ca.* Phytoplasma *solani*"

"*Ca.* Phytoplasma *spartii*"

"*Ca.* Phytoplasma *trifolii*"

"*Ca.* Phytoplasma *ulmi*"

"*Ca.* Phytoplasma *vitis*"

"*Ca.* Phytoplasma *ziziphi*"

Phytoplasma, formerly known as 'Mycoplasma-like organisms' or MLOs, are specialised bacteria that are obligate parasites of plant phloem tissue and of some insects. They were first discovered by scientists in 1967 when they were named mycoplasma-like organisms or MLOs. They cannot be cultured in vitro in cell-free media. They are characterised by their lack of a cell wall, a pleiomorphic or filamentous shape, normally with a diameter less than 1 micrometer, and their very small genomes.

Phytoplasmas are pathogens of important crops, including coconuts and sugarcane, causing a wide variety of symptoms that ranges from mild yellowing to death of infected plants. They are most prevalent in tropical and sub-tropical regions of the world. Phytoplasmas require a vector to be transmitted from plant to plant, and this normally takes the form of sap sucking insects such as leaf hoppers in which they are also able to replicate.

History

There are references to diseases now known to be caused by phytoplasmas as far back as 1603 for Mulberry dwarf disease in Japan Such diseases were originally thought to be caused by viruses, which, like phytoplasmas, require insect vectors, cannot be cultured, and have some symptom similarity. In 1967 phytoplasmas were discovered in ultrathin sections of plant phloem tissue and named mycoplasma-like organisms due to the fact that they physically resembled mycoplasmas The organisms were renamed phytoplasmas in 1994 at the 10th congress of the International Organization of Mycoplasmology.

Morphology

The cell membranes of all phytoplasmas studied so far usually contain a single immunodominant protein (of unknown function) that makes up the majority of the protein content of the cell membrane The typical phytoplasma exhibits a pleiomorphic or filamentous shape and is less than 1 micrometer in diameter. Like other prokaryotes, DNA is free in the cytoplasm. They are believed to reproduce through binary fission.

Symptoms

A common symptom caused by phytoplasma infection is phyllody, the production of leaf-like structures in place of flowers. Evidence suggests that the phytoplasma downregulates a gene involved in petal formation (*AP3* and its orthologues) and genes involved in the maintenance of the apical meristem (*Wus* and

CLV1) This causes sepals to form where petals should. Other symptoms, such as the yellowing of leaves, are thought to be caused by the phytoplasma's presence in the phloem, affecting its function and changing the transport of carbohydrates.

Phytoplasma infected plants may also suffer from virescence, the development of green flowers due to the loss of pigment in the petal cells. Sometimes sterility of the flowers is also seen. Many phytoplasma infected plants gain a bushy or witch's broom appearance due to changes in normal growth patterns caused by the infection. Most plants show apical dominance, but phytoplasma infection can cause the proliferation of auxiliary (side) shoots and an increase in size of the internodes Such symptoms are actually useful in the commercial production of poinsettia. The infection produces more axillary shoots, which enables production of poinsettia plants that have more than one flower. Phytoplasmas may cause many other symptoms that are induced because of the stress placed on the plant by infection rather than specific pathogenicity of the phytoplasma. Photosynthesis, especially photosystem II, is inhibited in many phytoplasma infected plants Phytoplasma infected plants often show yellowing which is caused by the breakdown of chlorophyll, whose biosynthesis is also inhibited.

Transmission

Movement Between Plants

The phytoplasmas are mainly spread by insects of the families Cicadellidea (leaf-hoppers) and Fulgoridea (planthoppers) which feed on the phloem tissues of infected plants, picking up the phytoplasmas and transmitting them to the next plant they feed on. For this reason the host range of phytoplasmas is strongly dependent upon its insect vector. Phytoplasmas contain a major antigenic protein that makes up the majority of their cell surface proteins. This protein has been shown to interact with insect microfilament complexes and is believed to be the determining factor in insect-phytoplasma interaction. Phytoplasmas may overwinter in insect vectors or perennial plants. Phytoplasmas can have varying effects on their insect hosts; examples of both reduced and increased fitness have been seen.

Phytoplasmas enter the insect's body through the stylet, move through the intestine, and are then absorbed into the haemolymph. From here they proceed to colonise the salivary glands, a process that can take up to three weeks. Once established, phytoplasmas will be found in most major organs of an infected insect host. The time between being taken up by the insect and reaching an infectious titre in the salivary glands is called the latency period. Phytoplasmas can also be spread via vegetative propagation such as the grafting of a piece of infected plant onto a healthy plant.

Movement within Plants

Phytoplasmas are able to move within the phloem from source to sink, and they are able to pass through sieve tube elements. But since they spread more slowly than solutes, for this and other reasons, movement by passive translocation is not supported

Detection and Diagnosis

Before molecular techniques were developed, the diagnosis of phytoplasma diseases was difficult because they could not be cultured. Thus classical diagnostic techniques, such as observation of symptoms, were used. Ultrathin sections of the phloem tissue from suspected phytoplasma infected plants would also be examined for their presence. Treating infected plants with antibiotics such as tetracycline to see if this cured the plant was another diagnostic technique employed. Molecular diagnostic techniques for the detection of phytoplasma began to emerge in the 1980s and included ELISA based methods. In the early 1990s, PCR-based methods were developed that were far more sensitive than those that used ELISA, and RFLP analysis allowed the accurate identification of different strains and species of phytoplasma.

More recently, techniques have been developed that allow for assessment of the level of infection. Both QPCR and bioimaging have been shown to be effective methods of quantifying the titre of phytoplasmas within the plant.

Control

Phytoplasmas are normally controlled by the breeding and planting of disease resistance varieties of crops (believed to the most economically viable option) and by the control of the insect vector. Tissue culture can be used to produce clones of phytoplasma infected plants that are healthy. The chances of gaining healthy plants in this manner can be enhanced by the use of cryotherapy, freezing the plant samples in liquid nitrogen, before using them for tissue culture. Work has also been carried out investigating the effectiveness of plantibodies targeted against phytoplasmas. Tetracyclines are bacteriostatic to phytoplasmas, that is they inhibit their growth. However, without continuous use of the antibiotic, disease symptoms will reappear. Thus, tetracycline is not a viable control agent in agriculture, but it is used to protect ornamental coconut trees.

Genetics

The genomes of three phytoplasmas have been sequenced: Aster Yellows Witches Broom Onion Yellows (*Ca.* Phytoplasma *asteris*) and *Ca.* Phytoplasma *australiense*. Phytoplasmas have very small genomes, which also have extremely low levels of the nucleotides G and C, sometimes as little as 23% which is thought to be the threshold for a viable genome In fact Bermuda grass white leaf phytoplasma has a genome size of just 530Kb, one of the smallest known genomes of living organisms. Larger phytoplasma genomes are around 1350 Kb. The small genome size associated with phytoplasmas is due to their being the product of reductive evolution from Bacillus/Clostridium ancestors. They have lost 75% or more of their original genes, and this is why they can no longer survive outside of insects or plant phloem. Some phytoplasmas contain extrachromosomal DNA such as plasmids.

Despite their very small genomes, many predicted genes are present in multiple copies. Phytoplasmas lack many genes for standard metabolic functions and have no functioning homologous recombination pathways, but do have a *sec* transport pathway. Phytoplasma genomes contain large numbers of transposon genes and insertion sequences. They also contain a unique family of repetitive extragenic palindromes (REPs) called PhREPS whose role is unknown though it is theorised that the stem loop structures the PhREPS are capable of forming may play a role in transcription termination or genome stability.

7

Plant Disease Control

Introduction

When a plant expert recommends that a certainchemical be used for plant disease control, heor she often refers to it by its common name. Butnot all product labels list the ingredients by their common names. Instead, they use chemical terminology. Consumers can become confused whentrying to find a chemical that was recommended by its common name but is listed on the product labels by its chemical term.

Besides the problem of identifying the right products, homeowners also face a declining number of disease-control products that are available in small packages. To get what they need, homeowners may eventually have to buy chemicals in larger quantities. This poses several problems.

Retailers and consumers can become confused when trying to find a particular product tocontrol a plant disease. The problems often arisewhen a specific chemical is recommended forcontrolling the disease, but the chemical is soldunder a variety of trade names:

- Larger packaging instructions seldom give rates in quantity per gallon, but instead in quantity per acre.
- Larger size containers cost more (even though the cost per unit used is less).

- Adequate space for storing excess chemicals may not be available.

To help consumers and retailers identify the products used to control plant diseases in Texas, a list of chemicals and the products available to homeowners is provided below. A survey was made to identify the chemical companies whose products are most commonly found in retail outlets in Texas. The products contained in this listing are the ones currently being formulated. Discontinued products and formulations are often available at retail outlets until supplies are exhausted. Not included are products normally packaged for agricultural use, even though some of these products are stocked in certain retail outlets. For example, copper hydroxide can be purchased in 2-pound bags under the trade name Kocide 101, but only the products sold in smaller quantities are listed here. Home owners can more easily determine what to buy if they understand what information is included on the product labels. Listed on every product label is the name of the active ingredient, which is the chemical that acts against the disease. The law requires that each product label include the chemistry terminology of the active ingredient. This terminology describes the chemical makeup of the compound.

Because chemical names are long and cumbersome to pronounce, each chemical has been assigned an official common name. For most people, it is easier to use the common name rather than the chemical name. Manufacturers are not required to put the common name on the label, but some do.

Common Name Chemical Name

Triadimefon 1-(4-chlorophenoxy)-3, 3- dimethyl-1-(1H-1,2,4- triazo-1-yl)-butanone Four tables are included in this publication to help homeowners and retailers distinguish among the products available. Table 6.1 lists common chemical names and the corresponding chemical name for each active ingredient. Table 6.2 lists all trade name products and product manufacturers for each chemical. Combination products, those containing more than one chemical, are included. In most cases, the additional chemicals are insecticides.

Table 6.2 also indicates ether a product can be used on at least one vegetable, one fruit or turf and/or one ornamental. Refer to the product labels for specific crops and instructions. Table 6.3 lists each product by company or brand name, with a reference number to Table 6.2. If you know the product name, use Table 3 to determine its location in Table 6.2, where the active ingredient is listed. Table 6.3 also serves as a reference to the various products sold under a given brand name.

Table 6.1: Plant disease control chemicals

Common Name	Chemical Name
1. Captan	N-trichloromethylthic-4-cyclohexene-1 2-dicarboximide
2. chitin (organic)	Poly-N-acetyl-D-glucosamine)-Protein
3. chlorothalonil	tetrachloroisophthalonitrile
4. copper ammonium complex	exact formula not known
5. copper hydroxide	copper hydroxide
6. copper salts	copper salts of fatty and resin acids
7. copper sulfate	copper sulfate penthaydrate
8. fosetyl-al	aluminum trio (O-ethyl phosphonate)
9. lime sulphur	calcium polysulfide
10. mancozeb	A coordination product of zinc ion and manganese ethylene bisdithocarbamete
11. maneb	manganese ethylene bisdithocarbamate
12. myclobutanil	alpha butyl-alpha 4-(chlorophenyl)-I H-1, 2 4-triazole-I-propanenitrile
13. neem oil (organic)	darified hydrophobic extract of neem oil
14. PCNB	pentachloronitrobenzene
15. Potassium bicarbonate	potassium bicarbonate
16. Propiconazole	I-(2-2, 4 -dichlorophenyl)-4-propyl-1, 3 dioxolan-2- ylmethyl)-IH-I, 2, 4-triazole
17. Quaternary ammonium compound	various forms of N-alkyl ammonium chloride
18. streptomycin sulfate	streptomycin sulfate
19. sulphur	sulphur

(Contd...)

Common Name	Chemical Name
20. tebuconazole	alpha-[2-(4-chlorophenyl)ethyl]-alpha-(I, I dimethylethyl)-IH-I, 2, 4-triazole-I ethanol
21. thiophanate methyl	dimethyl 4, 4-0-phenylenebis (3-thioallophanate)
22. thiram	tetramethylthiuram disulfide
23. triadimefon	I-(4-chlorophenoxy)-3, 3-dimethyl-I-I(IH-1, 2, 4-triazo-I-yl)-butanone
24. triforine	(N, N′ [1, 4 piperazinediylbis (2, 2, 2-trichloroethylidene)] bis [formamide])

Table 6.2: Trade and brand names of products containing the chemical ingredients listed in Table 6.1.

***V = Vegetable; F = Fruit; T/O = Turf/Ornament**

Common name/trade name	Brand name	V*	F*	T/O
1. **Captan**				
a. Captan Fungicide	Hi-Yield	seed tr	x	x
b. Captan Fruit and Ornamental	Bonide		x	x
Captan combination products				
c. Insecticide Miticide Fungicide (captain + carbaryl + malathion)	Bonide		x	x
d. Fruit Tree Spray (captan + malathion)	Forti-lome		x	
e. Liquid Fruit Tree Spray (captan + methoxyclor + carbaryl + malathion)	Dexol		x	
f. Fruit Tree Spray (captan + carbaryl + malathion)	Bonide		x	x
g. Rescue (captan + carbaryl + malathion)	Martin's		x	x
h. Rose Rx (captan+malathion+carbaryl)	Bonide		x	
2. **Chitin**				
a. Nem-A-Cide Nematode Control	Hi-Yield	x	x	x

(Contd...)

Common name/trade name	Brand name	V*	F*	T/O
3. Chlorothalonil				
a. Garden Disease Control	Ortho	x	x	x
b. Liquid Fungicide	Forti-lome	x		x
c. Daconil Lawn, Vegetable and Flower Fungicide	Hi-Yield	x		x
d. Fung-onil Concentrate	Bonide	x	x	x
e. Fung-onil (Ready-To-Use)	Bonide	x	x	x
f. Bravado Fungicide	Monterey	x	x	x
4. Copper ammonium complex				
a. Liqui-Cop	Monterey	x	x	x
5. Copper hydroxide				
a. Blackspot Powdery Mildew Control	Ferti-lome			x
b. Copper Fungicide	Hi-Yield	x		x
6. Copper salts				
a. Liquid Copper Fungicide	Bonide	x	x	x
b. Concern Copper Soap Fungicide	Concern	x	x	x
7. Copper sulfate				
a. Bordeaux Powder	Dexol	x	x	x
b. Copper Dust or Spray	Bonide	x	x	x
Copper sulfate combination products				
c. Bordeaux Mix Fungicide (copper sulfate + lime)	Hi-Yield	x	x	x
d. Dragon Dust with Copper (copper sulfate + carbaryl + rotenone)	Bonide	x		
e. Garden Dust (copper sulfate+rotenone)	Bonide	x	x	x
f. Rose and Flower Dust (copper sulfate+rotenone)	Greenlight			x
8. Fosetyl-Al				
a. Monterey Aliette	Monterey			x
9. Lime sulfur				
a. Lime-Sulfur Spray	Bonide		x	x
b. Lime sulphur Spray	Hi-Yield		x	x
Lime sulfur combination products				
c. Oil & Lime Sulfur Spray (lime sulfur + oil)	Bonide		x	x

(Contd...)

Common name/trade name	Brand name	V*	F*	T/O
10. Mancozeb				
a. Mancozeb Flowable	Bonide	x	x	
11. Maneb				
a. Maneb Garden Fungicide	Hi-Yield	x	x	
12. Myclobutanil				
a. Immunox Multi-Purpose Fungicide	Spectracide		x	x
b. Immunox Lawn Disease Control Systemic Fungicide Concentrate	Spectracide			x
c. Fung-Away Systemic Lawn Fungicide - Granular	Greenlight			x
d. F-Stop	Ferti-lome			x
myclobutanil combination products				
e. Immunox Insect and Disease Control (myclobutanil+permethrin)	Spectracide			x
f. Immunox Insect and Disease Control (aerosol)	Spectracide			x
13. Neem Oil				
a. Neem Concentrate	Green Light	x	x	x
b. Rose Rx 3-in-I	Bonide	x	x	x
c. Rose Defense	Green Light			x
d. Powdery Mildew Killer	Green Light	x	x	x
e. 70% Neem Oil	Monterey	x	x	x
f. Triple Action Plus	Ferti-lome	x	x	x
g. Rose Flower & Vegetable Spray	Ferti-lome	x		x
14. PCNB				
a. Terraclor Granular Fungicide	Hi-Yield			x
b. Turfcide 10G	Crompton			x
c. Turfcide 400 (Liquid)	Crompton			x
d. Turf and Ornamental Fungicide	Hi-Yield			x
PCNB combination products				
e. Azalea, Carnellia, Crepe Myrtle Spray (PCNB + malathion)	Forti-lome			x
f. Fungicide for Brown Patch (PCNB + fertilizer)	Ferti-lome			
15. Potassium bicarbonate				
a. Remedy	Bonide	x	x	x

(Contd...)

Common name/trade name	Brand name	V*	F*	T/O
16. Propiconazole				
a. Systemic Fungicide	Ferti-lome			x
b. Lawn Disease Control	Ortho			x
c. Infuse	Bonide			x
17. Quaternary ammonium compounds				
a. Consan 20	Hi-Yield			x
b. Consan Triple Action 20	Parkway			x
18. Streptomycin sulfate				
a. Fire Blight Spray	Ferti-lome		x	x
b. Fire Blight Spray	Bonide	x	x	
19. Sulphur				
a. Wettable Dusting Sulphur	Green Light	x	x	x
b. Dusting Sulphur	Ferti-lome	x	x	x
c. Dusting Wettable sulphur	Hi-Yield	x	x	x
d. Garden Fungicide	Safer	x	x	x
e. Sulfur Plant Fungicide	Bonide	x	x	x
20. Tebuconazole				
a. Disease Control for Roses, Flowers and Shrubs	Bayer Advanced			x
tebuconazole combination products				
b. All-in-One Rose & Flower Care (tebuconazole+imidacloprid+fertilizer)	Bayer Advanced			x
21. Thiophanate methyl				
a. Systemic Fungicide	Green Light			x
b. Halt Systemic Fungicide	Ferti-lome			x
c. Lawn Fungus Control	Scotts			x
22. Thiram				
a. Bonide Bulb Saver	Bonide			x
23. Triadimefon				
a. Fung-Away (Systemic Lawn Fungicide Spray)	Green Light			x
b. Fung-Away (Systemic Fungicide)	Green Light			x
c. Lawn Fungicide Granules	Hi-Yield			x
d. Fungus Control for Lawns	Bayer Advanced			x
e. Fungi-onil Lawn Disease Control	Bonide			x

(Contd...)

Common name/trade name	Brand name	V*	F*	T/O
24. **Triforine**				
a. Rose Pride Rose & Shrub Disease Control	Ortho			x
Triforine combination products				
b. Ortho Orthenex Garden Insect and Disease Control (trioforine + acephate + vendx®)	Ortho			x
c. Ortho Orthenex Garden Insect and Disease Control (aerosol) (triforine + acephate + resmethrin)	Ortho			x

Table 6.3: Index to plant disease control products in Table 6.2.

Brand name	Product name	Reference Table 2
Bayer Advanced Lawn	Fungus Control for Lawns	23-d
	Disease Control for Roses, Flowers and Shrubs	20-a
	All-In-One Rose and Flower Care (tebuconazole+ imidacloprid+fertilizer	20-b
Bonide	Bonide Bulb Saver	22-a
	Captan Fruit and Ornamental	1-b
	Liquid Copper Fungicide	6-a
	Copper Dust or Spray	7-b
	Fung-onil Concentrate	3-d
	Fung-onil (Ready-to-Use)	3-e
	Fung-onil Lawn Disease Control	23-e
	Lime Sulfur Spray	9-a
	Mancozeb Flowable	10-a
	Fire Blight Spray	18-b
	Remedy	15-a
	Sulfur Plant Fungicide	19-e
	Rose Rx 3-in-I	13-b
	Infuse	16-c
	Combination Products	
	Fruit Tree Spray (captan + malathion+ carbaryl)	1-f
	Insecticide Miticide Fungicide (captan + carbaryl + malathion)	1-c
	Rose Rx (captan+malathion+carbaryl)	1-h
	Dragon Dust with Copper (copper sulfate + carbaryl + rotenone)	7-d
	Garden Dust (copper sulfate + rotenone)	7-e
	Oil and Lime Sulfur Spray (lime sulfur + oil)	9-c

(Contd...)

Brand name	Product name	Reference Table 2
Concern	Concern Copper Soap Fungicide	6-b
Crompton	Turfcide 10G	14-b
	Turfcide 400 (liquid)	14-c
Dexol	Liquid Fruit Tree Spray	1-e
	Bordeaux Powder	7-a
Ferti-lome	Blackspot Powdery Mildew Control	5-a
	Dusting Sulphur	19-b
	Fire Blight Spray	18-a
	Halt Systemic Fungicide	21-b
	Liquid Fungicide	3-b
	F-Stop	12-d
	Triple Action Plus	13-f
	Rose Flower & Vegetable Spray	13-g
	Systemic Fungicide	16-a
	Combination Products	
	Azalea, Camellia, Crepe Myrtle Spray (PCNB + malathion)	14-c
	Fruit Tree Spray (captan + malathion)	1-d
	Fungicide for Brown Patch (PCNB + fertilizer)	14-f
Green Light	Fung-Away (Systemic Lawn Fungicide Spray)	23-a
	Fung-Away (Systemic Fungicide)	23-b
	Fung-Away (Systemic Lawn Fungicide-Granular)	12-c
	Systemic Fungicide	21-a
	Wettable Dusting Sulphur	19-a
	Neem Concentrate	13-a
	Rose Defense	13-c
	Powdery Mildew Killer	13-d
	Combination products	
	Rose & Flower Dust (copper sulfate + rotenone)	7-f
Hi-Yield	Daconil Lawn, Vegetable and Flower Fungicide	3-c
	Lawn Fungicide Granules	23-c
	Lime Sulphur Spray	9-b
	Maneb Garden Fungicide	11-a
	Terraclor Granular Fungicide	14-a
	Dusting Wettable Sulphur	19-c
	Nem-A Cide Nematode Control	2-a
	Copper Fungicide	5-a
	Captan Fungicide	1-a

(Contd...)

Brand name	Product name	Reference Table 2
	Consan 20	17-a
	Turf and Ornamental Fungicide	14-d
	Combination products	
	Bordeaux Mix Fungicide (copper sulfate + lime)	7-c
Martin's	Rescue (captan + carbaryl + malathion)	1-g
Monterey	Bravado Fungicide	3-f
	Monterey Aliette	8-a
	Liqui-Cop	4-a
	70% Neem Oil	13-e
Ortho	Rose Pride Rose & Shrub Disease Control	24-a
	Garden Disease Control	3-a
	Lawn Disease Control	16-b
	Combination products	
	Ortho Orthenex (triforine + acephate + vendex®)	24-b
	Ortho Orthenex (aerosol) (triforine +acephate + resmethrin)	24-c
Parkway	Consan Triple Action 20	17-b
Safer	Garden Fungicide	19-d
Scotts	Lawn Fungus Control	21-c
Spectracide	Immunox Multi-Purpose Fungicide	12-a
	Immunox Lawn Disease Control Systemic Fungicide Concentrate	12-b
	Combination products	
	Immunox Insect and Disease Control (myclobutanil + permethrin)	12-e
	Immunox Insect and Disease Control (aerosol) (myclobutanil + permethrin)	12-f

8

Trap Crop

Introduction

A trap crop is a plant that attracts parasitic insects away from attacking nearby crops. This form of companion planting can save the main target of agriculture from decimation by pests without the potential issues and controversy involved in using pesticides. Trap crops can be planted around the circumference of the field to be protected, or interspersed among them, for example being planted every ninth row. Trap crops are, when used on an industrial scale, generally planted at a key time in the pest's lifecycle, and then destroyed before that lifecycle finishes and the pest might have transferred from the trap plants to the main crop. Examples of trap crops include:

- Alfalfa planted in strips among cotton, to draw away lygus bugs, while castor beans surround the field, or tobacco in is planted in strips among it, to protect from heliotis.
- Rose enthusiasts often plant geraniums among their rosebushes because japanese beetles are drawn to the geraniums, which are toxic to them.
- Chervil is used by gardeners to protect vegetable plants from slugs.
- Rye, sesbania, and sicklepod are used to protect soybeans from corn seeding maggots, stink bugs, and velvet green caterpillars, respectively.

The Science of Trap Crops

Recent studies on host-plant finding have shown that flying pests are far less successful if their host-plants are surrounded by any other plant, or even "decoy-plants" made of green plastic, cardboard or any other green material. The host-plant finding process occurs in three phases. The first phase is stimulation by odours characteristic to the host-plant. This induces the insect to try and land on the plant it seeks. But insects avoid landing on brown (bare) soil. So if only the host-plant is present, the insects will quasi systematically find it by simply landing on the only green thing around. This is called an "appropriate landing". When it does an "inappropriate landing", it flies off to any other nearby patch of green. It eventually leaves the area if there are too many 'inappropriate' landings. The second phase of host-plant finding is for the insect to make short flights from leaf to leaf to assess the plant's overall suitability. The number of leaf-to-leaf flights varies according to the insect species and to the host-plant stimulus received from each leaf. But the insect must accumulate sufficient stimuli from the host-plant to lay eggs; so it must make a certain number of consecutive 'appropriate' landings.

Hence if it makes an 'inappropriate landing', the assessment of that plant is negative and the insect must start the process anew. Thus, it was shown that Clover used as a ground cover had the same disruptive effect on eight pest species from four different insect orders. An experiment showed that 36% of cabbage root flies laid eggs beside cabbages growing in bare soil (which resulted in no crop), compared to only 7% beside cabbages growing in clover (which allowed a good crop). Also that simple decoys made of greencard disrupted appropriate landings just as well as did the live ground cover. This is one of the reasons why monoculture is counter-productive, the pesticides effectively immunizing the pests more and more generation after generation, while still providing ample shelter and food for these.

Companion Planting

Companion planting in gardening and agriculture is planting of different crops in close physical proximity, on the theory that they will help each other. It is a form of polyculture. Companion planting is used by farmers and gardeners in both industrialized and developing countries. Many of the modern principles of companion planting were present many centuries ago in the cottage garden. Although there is a wealth of information on its historic use, there remains limited available scientific research on the effectiveness for each of these interventions.

For farmers, these techniques are used in Integrated Pest Management, and systems can be set up to allow the farmer to have more yield and/or reduce pesticides. In the developing world, tropical crops are used instead of temperate ones and provide NGOs and other organizations a tool for alleviating poverty. For gardeners, the combinations of plants also make for a more varied, attractive vegetable garden. It can also be used to mitigate the decline of biodiversity. Companion planting was widely touted in the 1970s as part of the organic gardening movement. It was encouraged not for pragmatic reasons like trellising, but rather with the idea that different species of plant may thrive more when close together. It is also a technique frequently used in permaculture, together with mulching, polyculture, and changing of crops.

One traditional practice was planting of corn (maize) and pole beans together. The cornstalk would serve as a trellis for the beans to climb while the beans would fix nitrogen for the corn. The inclusion of squash with these two plants completes the Three Sisters technique, pioneered by Native American peoples. Nasturtium are well-known to attract caterpillars, so planting them alongside or around vegetables such as lettuce or cabbage will protect them, as the egg-laying insects will tend to prefer the nasturtium. This is called a 'trap crop'.

Crops that suffer from greenfly and other aphids may benefit from the proximity of marigolds: These smell bad to aphids and attract hoverflies, a predator of aphids, and are also said to deter other pests.

The use of plants that produce copious nectar and protein-rich pollen in a vegetable garden (insectary plants) is a good way to enhance the population of beneficial insects that control pests. Some insects in the adult form are nectar or pollen feeders, while in the larval form they are voracious predators of pest insects.

There are a number of systems and ideas using companion planting. Square foot gardening, for example, attempts to protect plants from many normal gardening problems by packing them as closely together as possible, which is facilitated by using companion plants, which can be closer together than normal.

Another system using companion planting is the forest garden, where companion plants are intermingled to create an actual ecosystem, emulating the interaction of up to seven levels of plants in a forest or woodland. Organic gardening often depends on companion planting for its best performance, since so many synthetic means of fertilizing, weed reduction, pest control, and other garden needs are forbidden.

Good Weeds

There are many beneficial weeds, which can be allowed to grow alongside plants, imparting the same kinds of benefits as mixing cultivated crops.

Host-finding Disruption

Recent studies on host-plant finding have shown that flying pests are far less successful if their host-plants are surrounded by any other plant or even "decoy-plants" made of green plastic, cardboard, or any other green material.

The host-plant finding process occurs in phases:

- The first phase is stimulation by odours characteristic to the host-plant. This induces the insect to try to land on the plant it seeks. But insects avoid landing on brown (bare) soil. So if only the host-plant is present, the insects will quasi-systematically find it by simply landing on the only green thing around. This is called (from the point of view of the insect) "appropriate landing". When it does an "inappropriate landing," it flies off to any other nearby patch of green. It eventually leaves the area if there are too many 'inappropriate' landings.

- The second phase of host-plant finding is for the insect to make short flights from leaf to leaf to assess the plant's overall suitability. The number of leaf-to-leaf flights varies according to the insect species and to the host-plant stimulus received from each leaf. The insect must accumulate sufficient stimuli from the host-plant to lay eggs; so it must make a certain number of consecutive 'appropriate' landings. Hence if it makes an 'inappropriate landing', the assessment of that plant is negative, and the insect must start the process anew.

Thus it was shown that clover used as a ground cover had the same disruptive effect on eight pest species from four different insect orders. An experiment showed that 36% of cabbage root flies laid eggs beside cabbages growing in bare soil (which resulted in no crop), compared to only 7% beside cabbages growing in clover (which allowed a good crop). Simple decoys made of green cardboard also disrupted appropriate landings just as well as did the live ground cover. This is one of the reasons why monoculture is counter-productive: pesticides effectively immunized the pests more and more, generation after generation, while still providing ample shelter and food for these.

Companion Plant Categories

Companion plants can benefit each other in a number of different ways, including:

- *Flavor enhancement:* some plants, especially herbs, seem to subtly change the flavor of other plants around them.
- *Hedged investment:* multiple plants in the same space increase the odds of some yield being given, even if one category encounters catastrophic issues.
- *Level interaction:* plants that grow on different levels in the same space, perhaps providing ground cover or working as a trellis for another plant.
- *Nitrogen fixation:* plants that fix nitrogen in the ground, making it available to other plants.
- *Pest suppression:* plants that repel insects, plants, or other pests like nematodes or fungi, through chemical means.

- ***Positive hosting:*** attracts or is inhabited by beneficial insects or other organisms which benefit plants, as with ladybugs or some "good nematodes".
- ***Protective shelter:*** one type of plant may serve as a wind break or shade for another.
- ***Trap cropping:*** plants that attract pests away from others.
- ***Pattern disruption:*** with monocultural crops, pests can quickly and easily spread from one plant to the next. Companion plants interrupt this spread.

Alfalfa

Alfalfa (*Medicago sativa*) is a flowering plant in the pea family Fabaceae cultivated as an important forage crop. In the U.K. it is known as lucerne and Lucerne grass in south Asia.

Alfalfa is a cool season perennial legume living from three to twelve years, depending on variety and climate. It resembles clover with clusters of small purple flowers. The plant grows to a height of up to 1 metre (3 ft), and has a deep root system sometimes stretching to 4.5 metres (15 ft). This makes it very resilient, especially to droughts. It has a tetraploid genome. The plant exhibits autotoxicity, which means that it is difficult for alfalfa seed to grow in existing stands of alfalfa. Therefore, it is recommended that alfalfa fields be rotated with other species (e.g. corn, wheat) before reseeding.

Like other legumes, its root nodules contain bacteria, *Sinorhizobium meliloti*, with the ability to fix nitrogen, producing a high-protein feed regardless of available nitrogen in the soil. Its nitrogen-fixing abilities (which increases soil nitrogen) and use as animal feed greatly improved agricultural efficiency. (The nitrogen comes from the air, which is 78 per cent molecular nitrogen.)

Alfalfa is widely grown throughout the world as forage for cattle, and is most often harvested as hay, but can also be made into silage, grazed, or fed as greenchop. Alfalfa has the highest feeding value of all common hay crops, being used less frequently as pasture. When grown on soils where it is well-adapted, alfalfa is the highest yielding forage plant.

Alfalfa is one of the most important legumes used in agriculture. The US is the largest alfalfa producer in the world, but considerable area is found in Argentina (primarily grazed), Australia, South Africa, and the Middle East. Known as Kuthirai Masal in Tamil, alfalfa is mostly grown in the Coimbatore district of Tamil Nadu, southern India.

The leading alfalfa growing States (within the U.S.A.) are California, South Dakota, and Wisconsin. The upper Midwestern states account for about 50% of US production, the Northeastern states 10%, the Western States 40% and the Southeastern states almost none. Alfalfa has a wide range of adaptation and can be grown from very cold northern plains to high mountain valleys, from rich temperate agricultural regions to Mediterranean climates and searing hot deserts.

Its primary use is as feed for dairy cattle (Because of its high protein), and secondarily for beef cattle, horses, sheep, and goats. Humans also eat alfalfa sprouts, in salads and sandwiches, for example. Tender shoots are eaten in some places as a leaf vegetable. Human consumption of fresh mature plant parts is rare and limited primarily by alfalfa's high fiber content. Dehydrated alfalfa leaf is commercially available as a dietary supplement in several forms, such as tablets, powders and tea. Alfalfa is believed by some to be a galactagogue, a substance that induces lactation.

Culture

Alfalfa can be sown in spring or fall, and does best on well-drained soils with a neutral pH of 6.8-7.5. Alfalfa requires a great deal of potassium. Alfalfa is moderately sensitive to salt levels in both the soil and irrigation water, although it continues to be grown in the arid southwest, where salinity is an emerging issue. Soils low in fertility should be fertilized with manure or a chemical fertilizer, but correction of pH is particularly important. Usually a seeding rate of 13-20 kg/hectare (12-25 lb/acre) is recommended, with differences based upon region, soil type, and seeding method. A nurse crop is sometimes used, particularly for spring plantings, to reduce weed problems. Herbicides are sometimes used instead, particularly in Western production.

In most climates, alfalfa is cut three to four times a year but is harvested up to 12 times per year in Arizona and Southern California. Total yields are typically around 8 tonnes per hectare (4 short tons per acre) but yields have been recorded up to 20 t/ ha (16 short tons per acre). Yields vary with region, weather, and the crop's stage of maturity when cut. Later cuttings improve yield but reduce nutritional content. Alfalfa leafcutter bee, *Megachile rotundata*, a pollinator on alfalfa flower.

Alfalfa is considered an 'insectary' due to the large number of insects it attracts. Some pests such as Alfalfa weevil, aphids, armyworms, and the potato leafhopper can reduce alfalfa yields dramatically, particularly with the second cutting when weather is warmest. Chemical controls are sometimes used to prevent this. Alfalfa is also susceptible to root rots including phytophora, rhizoctonia, and Texas Root Rot.

Alfalfa seed production requires the presence of pollinators when the fields of alfalfa are in bloom. Alfalfa pollination is somewhat problematic, however, because the pollen-carrying keel of the flower trips and strikes pollinating bees on the head to help transfer the pollen to the foraging bee. Western honey bees do not like being struck in the head repeatedly and learn to defeat this action by drawing nectar from the side of the flower. The bees thus collect the nectar but carry no pollen and so do not pollenate the next flower they visit. Because older, experienced bees don't pollinate alfalfa well, most pollination is accomplished by young bees that have not yet learned the trick of robbing the flower without tripping the head-knocking keel. When western honey bees are used to pollinate alfalfa, the beekeeper stocks the field at a very high rate to maximize the number of young bees. Today the alfalfa leafcutter bee is increasingly used to circumvent this problem. As a solitary but gregarious bee species, it does not build colonies or store honey, but is a very efficient pollinator of alfalfa flowers. Nesting is in individual tunnels in wooden or plastic material, supplied by the alfalfa seed growers. The leafcutter bees are used in the Pacific Northwest, while western honeybees dominate in California alfalfa seed production. A smaller amount of alfalfa produced for seed is pollinated by the alkali bee, mostly in the northwestern USA. It is cultured in special beds near the fields. These bees also have their own problems. They are not portable like honey bees; and when fields are planted in new areas, the bees take several seasons to build up. Honey bees are still trucked to many of the fields at bloom time.

Harvesting

When alfalfa is to be used as hay, it is usually cut and baled. Loose haystacks are still used in some areas, but bales are easier to transport and store. Ideally, the hay is cut just as the field is beginning to flower. When using farm equipment rather than hand-harvesting, a swather cuts the alfalfa and arranges it in windrows. In areas where the alfalfa does not immediately dry out on its own, a machine know as a mower-conditioner is used to cut the hay. The mower-conditioner has a set of rollers or flails that crimp and break the stems as they pass through the mower, making the alfalfa dry faster. After the alfalfa has dried, a tractor pulling a baler collects the hay into bales.

There are several types of bales commonly used for alfalfa. For small animals and individual horses, the alfalfa is baled into small "square" bales — actually rectangular, and typically about 40 x 45 x 100 cm (14 in x 18 in x 38 in). Small square bales weigh from 25 – 30 kg (50 – 70 pounds) depending on moisture, and can be easily hand separated into "flakes". Cattle ranches use large round bales, typically 1.4 to 1.8 m (4 to 6 feet) in diameter and weighing from 500 to 1,000 kg, (1000 to 2000 lb). These bales can be placed in stable stacks or in large feeders for herds of horses, or unrolled on the ground for large herds of cattle. The bales can be loaded and stacked with a tractor using a spike, known as a bale spear, that pierces the center of the bale. Or they can be handled with a grapple (claw) on the tractor's front-end loader. A more recent innovation is large "square" bales, roughly the same proportions as the small squares, but much larger. The bale size was set so that stacks would fit perfectly on a large flatbed truck. These are more common in western states.

When used as feed for dairy cattle alfalfa is often made into haylage by a process known as ensiling. Rather than drying it to make dry hay, the alfalfa is chopped finely and fermented in silos, trenches, or bags, anywhere where the oxygen supply can be limited to promote fermentation. Fermenting the alfalfa allows it to retain high nutrient levels similar to those of fresh forage, and is also more palatable to dairy cattle than dry hay.

Varieties

Considerable research and development has been done with this important plant. Older cultivars such as 'Vernal' have been the standard for years, but many better public and private varieties are now available and better adapted to particular climates. Private companies release many new varieties each year in the U.S.

Most varieties go dormant in the fall, with reduced growth in response to low temperatures and shorter days. 'Non-dormant' varieties that grow through the winter are planted in long-seasoned environments such as Mexico, Arizona, and Southern California, whereas 'dormant' varieties are planted in the Upper Midwest, Canada, and the Northeast. 'Non-dormant' varieties can be higher yielding, but they are susceptible to winter-kill in cold climates and have poorer persistence.

Most alfalfa cultivars contain genetic material from Sickle Medick (*M. falcata*), a wild variety of alfalfa that naturally hybridizes with *M. sativa* to produce Sand Lucerne (*M. sativa* ssp. *varia*). This species may bear either the purple flowers of alfalfa or the yellow of sickle medick, and is so called for its ready growth in sandy soil. Most of the improvements in alfalfa over the last decades have consisted of better disease resistance on poorly drained soils in wet years, better ability to overwinter in cold climates, and the production of more leaves. Multileaf alfalfa varieties have more than three leaflets per leaf, giving them greater nutritional content by weight because there is more leafy matter for the same amount of stem. Modern alfalfa varieties have probably a wider range of insect, disease, and nematode resistance than many other agricultural species. The North American Alfalfa Improvement Conference records new varieties and encourages communication between breeders.

Roundup Ready alfalfa is a genetically modified variety, patented by Monsanto, that is resistant to Monsanto's glyphosate herbicide Roundup. Although most broadleaf plants, including ordinary alfalfa, are sensitive to Roundup, growers can spray fields of Roundup Ready alfalfa with Roundup, and so kill the weeds without harming the alfalfa crop. Roundup Ready alfalfa was sold in the United States from 2005-2007 and more than 300,000 acres (1,200 km^2) were planted with it, out of 21,000,000 acres (85,000 km^2). However, in May 2007, the California Northern District Court issued an injunction order prohibiting farmers from planting Roundup Ready alfalfa until the US Department of Agriculture (USDA) completed a study on the genetically engineered crop's likely environmental impact. In response, the USDA put a hold on any further planting of Roundup Ready alfalfa. The key issues of the lawsuit were the possibility that Roundup Resistance could be transmitted to other plants, including both other crops and weeds, making major pest species resistant to an important herbicide, Roundup.

Phytoestrogens in Alfalfa

Alfalfa, like other leguminous crops, is a known source of phytoestrogens. Grazing on alfalfa has been suspected as a cause of reduced fertility in sheep.

Medical Uses

Alfalfa has been used as an herbal medicine for over 1,500 years. Alfalfa is high in protein, calcium, plus other minerals, vitamin A, vitamins in the B group, vitamin C, vitamin D, vitamin E, and vitamin K.

Traditional Uses

In early Chinese medicines, physicians used young alfalfa leaves to treat disorders related to the digestive tract and the kidneys. In Hindu societies, ayurvedic physicians used the leaves for treating poor digestion. They made a cooling poultice from the seeds for boils. At the time, alfalfa was also believed to be helpful towards people suffering from arthritis and water retention.

Modern Use

It is majorly used in homeopathic medicines worldwide. Today, alfalfa is suggested for treating anemia, diabetes, to extend appetite and contribute towards weight gain, as a diuretic for increased urination, for indigestion and bladder disorders, alfalfa can also be used as an estrogen replacement in order to increase breast milk and to mitigate premenstrual syndrome, a dietary supplement, and to lower blood cholestrol levels. Use in Organic Gardening

Alfalfa is commonly used as plant fertilizer in the form of granular pellets. Alfalfa is also used to make Alfalfa tea, which contains Triacontanol, a plant growth stimulant.

CHERVIL

Chervil (*Anthriscus cerefolium*) is a delicate annual herb related to parsley. Sometimes called garden chervil, it is used to season mild-flavoured dishes and is a constituent of the French herb mixture fines herbes.

A member of the Apiaceae, chervil is native to the Caucasus but was spread by the Romans through most of Europe, where it is now naturalised.

The plants grow to 40-70cm, with tripinnate leaves that may be curly. The small white flowers form small umbels, 2.5-5cm across. The fruit is about 1cm long, oblong-ovoid with a slender, ridged beak.

Root Chervil

Another type of chervil is grown as a root vegetable, sometimes called turnip rooted chervil or tuberous-rooted chervil. This type of chervil produces much thicker roots than types cultivated for their leaves. It was once a popular vegetable in the 19th century. It is now virtually forgotten and is little known in Britain and the United States, root chervil is very common in French cuisine, where it is used in most soups or stews.

Though it looks similar to parsnip it tastes quite different. Parsnips are among the closest relatives of parsley in the umbellifer family of herbs, although the similarity of the names is a coincidence, parsnip meaning "forked turnip". It is not related to real turnips. Chervil garnishing a salad.

Sometimes referred to as "gourmet's parsley", chervil is used to season poultry, seafood, and young vegetables. It is particularly popular in France, where it is added to omelettes, salads and soups. More delicate than parsley, it has a faint taste of liquorice.

Horticulture

Chervil is sometimes used as a trap crop by gardeners to protect vegetable plants from slugs.

Medical

Chervil had various traditional uses. Pregnant women bathed in an infusion of it; a lotion of it was used as a skin cleanser; and it was used medicinally as a blood purifier.

Cultivation

Chervil grows to a height of 12 to 26 inches. Chervil prefers a cool and moist location, otherwise it rapidly goes to seed.

Rose

A rose is a perennial flowering shrub or vine of the genus *Rosa*, within the family Rosaceae, that contains over 100 species. The species form a group of erect shrubs, and climbing or trailing plants, with stems that are often armed with sharp thorns. Most are native to Asia, with smaller numbers of species native to Europe, North America, and northwest Africa. Natives, cultivars and hybrids are all widely grown for their beauty and fragrance.

The leaves are alternate and pinnately compound, with sharply toothed oval-shaped leaflets. The plants fleshy edible fruit is called a rose hip. Rose plants range in size from tiny, miniature roses, to climbers that can reach 20 metres in height. Species from different parts of the world easily hybridize, which has given rise to the many types of garden roses. The name originates from Latin *rosa*, borrowed through Oscan from colonial Greek in southern Italy: *rhodon* (Aeolic form: *wrodon*), from Aramaic *wurrda*, from Assyrian *wurtinnu*, from Old Iranian *warda* (cf. Armenian *vard*, Avestan *warda*, Sogdian *ward*, Parthian *wâr*). Attar of rose is the steam-extracted essential oil from rose flowers that has been used in perfumes for centuries. Rose water, made from the rose oil, is widely used in Asian and Middle Eastern cuisine. Rose hips are occasionally made into jam, jelly, and marmalade, or are brewed for tea, primarily for their high Vitamin C content. They are also pressed and filtered to make rose hip syrup. Rose hips are also used to produce Rose hip seed oil, which is used in skin products.

Rosa Canina Hips

The leaves of most species are 5–15 centimetres long, pinnate, with (3–) 5–9 (–13) leaflets and basal stipules; the leaflets usually have a serrated margin, and often a few small prickles on the underside of the stem. The vast majority of roses are deciduous, but a few (particularly in Southeast Asia) are evergreen or nearly so.

The flowers of most species roses have five petals, with the exception of *Rosa sericea*, which usually has only four. Each petal is divided into two distinct lobes and is usually white or pink, though in a few species yellow or red. Beneath the petals are five sepals (or in the case of some Rosa sericea, four). These may be long enough to be visible when viewed from above and appear as green points alternating with the rounded petals. The ovary is inferior, developing below the petals and sepals.

The aggregate fruit of the rose is a berry-like structure called a rose hip. Rose species that produce open-faced flowers are attractive to pollinating bees and other insects, thus more apt to produce hips. Many of the domestic cultivars are so tightly petalled that they do not provide access for pollination. The hips of most species are red, but a few (e.g. *Rosa pimpinellifolia*) have dark purple to black hips. Each hip comprises an outer fleshy layer, the hypanthium, which contains 5–160 "seeds" (technically dry single-seeded fruits called achenes) embedded in a matrix of fine, but stiff, hairs. Rose hips of some species, especially the Dog Rose (*Rosa canina*) and Rugosa Rose (*Rosa rugosa*), are very rich in vitamin C, among the richest sources of any plant. The hips are eaten by fruit-eating birds such as thrushes and waxwings, which then disperse the seeds in their droppings. Some birds, particularly finches, also eat the seeds.

While the sharp objects along a rose stem are commonly called "thorns", they are actually prickles — outgrowths of the epidermis (the outer layer of tissue of the stem). True thorns, as produced by e.g. *Citrus* or *Pyracantha*, are modified stems, which always originate at a node and which have nodes and internodes along the length of the thorn itself. Rose prickles are typically sickle-shaped hooks, which aid the rose in hanging onto other vegetation when growing over it. Some species such as *Rosa rugosa* and *R. pimpinellifolia* have densely packed straight spines, probably an adaptation to reduce browsing by animals, but also possibly an adaptation to trap wind-blown sand and so reduce erosion and protect their roots (both of these species grow naturally on coastal sand dunes). Despite the presence of prickles, roses are frequently browsed by deer. A few species of roses only have vestigial prickles that have no points.

Species

Rosa multiflora are as follows:

Some representative rose species

- *Rosa canina*: Dog Rose, Briar Bush
- *Rosa chinensis*: China Rose
- *Rosa dumalis*: Glaucous Dog Rose
- *Rosa gallica*: Gallic Rose, French Rose
- *Rosa gigantea* (syn. *R. x odorata gigantea*)
- *Rosa glauca* (syn. *R. rubrifolia*): Redleaf Rose
- *Rosa laevigata* (syn. *R. sinica*): Cherokee Rose, Camellia Rose, Mardan Rose
- *Rosa majalis*: Cinnamon Rose
- *Rosa multiflora*: Multiflora Rose
- *Rosa persica* (syn. *Hulthemia persica, R. simplicifolia*)
- *Rosa pimpinellifolia*: Scotch Rose
- *Rosa roxburghii*: Chestnut Rose, Burr Rose
- *Rosa rubiginosa* (syn. *R. eglanteria*): Eglantine, Sweet Brier

- *Rosa rugosa*: Rugosa Rose, Japanese Rose
- *Rosa stellata*: Gooseberry Rose, Sacramento Rose
- *Rosa virginiana* (syn. *R. lucida*): Virginia Rose

Pests and Diseases

Roses are subject to several diseases, such as rose rust (*Phragmidium mucronatum*), rose black spot, and powdery mildew. Fungal diseases in the rose are best solved by a preventative fungicidal spray program rather than by trying to cure an infection after it emerges on the plant. After the disease is visible, its spread can be minimized through pruning and the use of fungicides, although the actual infection cannot be reversed. Certain rose varieties are considerably less susceptible than others to fungal diseases.

The main insect pest affecting roses is the aphid (greenfly), which sucks the sap and weakens the plant. (Ladybirds are a predator of aphids and should be encouraged in the rose garden.) The spraying with insecticide of roses is often recommended but should be done with care to minimize the loss of beneficial insects. Roses are also used as food plants by the larvae of some Lepidoptera (butterfly and moth) species; see list of Lepidoptera that feed on roses.

Cultivation

Roses are popular garden shrubs, as well as the most popular and commonly sold florists' flowers. In addition to their great economic importance as a florists crop, roses are also of great value to the perfume industry.

Many thousands of rose hybrids and cultivars have been bred and selected for garden use; most are double-flowered with many or all of the stamens having mutated into additional petals. As long ago as 1840 a collection numbering over one thousand different cultivars, varieties and species was possible when a rosarium was planted by Loddiges nursery for Abney Park Cemetery, an early Victorian garden cemetery and arboretum in England.

Twentieth-century rose breeders generally emphasized size and colour, producing large, attractive blooms with little or no scent. Many wild and "old-fashioned" roses, by contrast, have a strong sweet scent.

Roses thrive in temperate climates, though certain species and cultivars can flourish in sub-tropical and even tropical climates, especially when grafted onto appropriate rootstock.

There is no single system of classification for garden roses. In general, however, roses are placed in one of three main groups:

Wild Roses

The wild roses includes the species listed above and some of their hybrids.

Old Garden Roses

In general, Old Garden Roses of European or Mediterranean origin are once-blooming shrubs, with notably fragrant, double-flowered blooms primarily in shades of white, pink and red. The shrubs' foliage tends to be highly disease-resistant, and they generally bloom only on two-year-old canes.

Alba

Rosa x *alba* 'Alba Semiplena', an Alba rose

Rosa 'Maiden's Blush', an Alba rose

Literally "white roses", derived from *R. arvensis* and the closely allied *R. alba*. These are some of the oldest garden roses, probably brought to Great Britain by the Romans. The shrubs flower once yearly in the spring with blossoms of white or pale pink. The shrubs frequently feature gray-green foliage and a climbing habit of growth . Examples: 'Alba Semiplena', 'White Rose of York'.

Gallica

The gallica roses have been developed from *R. gallica*, which is a native of central and southern Europe. They flower once in the summer over low shrubs rarely over 4' tall. Unlike most other once-blooming Old Garden Roses, the gallica class includes shades of red, maroon and deep purplish crimson. Examples: 'Cardinal de Richelieu', 'Charles de Mills', 'Rosa Mundi' (*R. gallica versicolor*).

Damask

Robert de Brie is given credit for bringing damask roses from Persia to Europe sometime between 1254 and 1276, although there is evidence from ancient Roman frescoes that at least one damask rose, the Autumn Damask, existed in Europe for hundreds of years prior. Summer damasks (crosses between gallica roses and *R. phoenicea*) bloom once in summer. Autumn damasks (Gallicas crossed with *R. moschata*) bloom again later, in the autumn. Shrubs tend to have rangy to sprawly growth habits and vicious thorns. The flowers typically have a more loose petal formation than gallicas, as well as a stronger, tangy fragrance. Examples: 'Ispahan', 'Madame Hardy'.

Centifolia or Provence

Centifolia roses, raised in the seventeenth century in the Netherlands, are named for their "one hundred" petals; they are often called "cabbage" roses due to the globular shape of the flowers. The result of damask roses crossed with albas, the centifolias are all once-flowering. As a class, they are notable for their inclination to produce mutations of various sizes and forms, including moss roses and some of the first miniature roses (see below). Examples: 'Centifolia', 'Paul Ricault'.

Moss

Moss roses are cherised for this unique trait, but as a group they have contributed nothing to the development of new rose classifications. Moss roses with centifolia background are once-flowering; some moss roses exhibit repeat-blooming, indicative of Autumn Damask parentage. Example: 'Common Moss' (centifolia-moss), 'Alfred de Dalmas' (Autumn Damask moss).

China

The China roses were grown in East Asia for thousands of years and finally reached Western Europe in the late 1700s. Compared to the aforementioned European rose classes, the

Chinese roses had smaller, less fragrant, more poorly formed blooms carried over twiggier, more cold-sensitive shrubs. Yet they possessed the amazing ability to bloom repeatedly throughout the summer and into late autumn, unlike their European counterparts. This made them highly desirable for hybridization purposes in the early 1800s. The flowers of China roses were also notable for their tendency to "suntan," or darken over time — unlike the blooms of European roses, which tended to fade after opening. Four China roses ('Slater's Crimson China', 1792; 'Parsons' Pink China', 1793; 'Hume's Blush China', 1809; and 'Parks' Yellow Tea Scented China', 1824) were brought to Europe in the late eighteenth and early nineteenth centuries. This brought about the creation of the first classes of repeat-flowering Old Garden Roses, and later the Modern Garden Roses. Examples: 'Old Blush China', 'Mutabilis'.

Portland

The Portland roses represent the first group of crosses between China roses and European roses, specifically gallicas and damasks. They were named after the Duchess of Portland who received (from Italy in 1800) a rose then known as *R. paestana* or 'Scarlet Four Seasons' Rose' (now known simply as 'The Portland Rose'). The whole class of Portland roses was thence developed from that one rose. The first repeat-flowering class of rose with fancy European-style blossoms, they are mostly descended from hybrids between damask and China roses. The plants tend to be fairly short and shrubby, with proportionately short flower stalks. Example: 'James Veitch', 'Rose de Rescht', 'Comte de Chambourd'.

Bourbon

Bourbons originated on off the coast of Madagascar in the Indian Ocean. They are most likely the result of a cross between the Autumn Damask and the 'Old Blush' China rose, both of which were frequently used as hedging materials on the island. They flower repeatedly over vigorous, frequently semi-climbing shrubs with glossy foliage and purple-tinted canes. They were first Introduced in France in 1823. Examples: 'Louise Odier', 'Mme. Pierre Oger', 'Zéphirine Drouhin'.

Noisette

The first Noisette rose was raised as a hybrid seedling by a South Carolina rice planter named John Champneys. Its parents were the China Rose 'Parson's Pink' and the autumn-flowering musk rose (*Rosa moschata*), resulting in a vigorous climbing rose producing huge clusters of small pink flowers from spring to fall. Champneys sent seedlings of his rose (called 'Champneys' Pink Cluster') to his gardening friend, Philippe Noisette, who in turn sent plants to his brother Louis in Paris, who then introduced 'Blush Noisette' in 1817. The first Noisettes were small-blossomed, fairly winter-hardy climbers, but later infusions of Tea rose genes created a Tea-Noisette subclass with larger flowers, smaller clusters, and considerably reduced winter hardiness. Examples: 'Blush Noisette', 'Mme. Alfred Carriere' (Noisette), 'Marechal Niel' (Tea-Noisette). (See French and German articles on Noisette roses)

Tea

The teas are repeat-flowering roses, named for their fragrance being reminiscent of Chinese black tea (although this is not always the case). The color range includes pastel shades of white, pink and yellow, and the petals tend to roll back at the edges, producing a petal with a pointed tip. The individual flowers of many cultivars are semi-pendent and nodding, due to weak flower stalks. Examples: 'Lady Hillingdon', 'Maman Cochet'.

Hybrid Perpetual

The dominant class of roses in Victorian England, hybrid perpetuals first emerged in 1838 and were derived to a great extent from the Bourbons. They became the most popular garden and florist roses of northern Europe at the time, as the tender tea roses would not thrive in cold climates. The "perpetual" in the name hints at repeat-flowering, but many varieties of this class had poor reflowering habits; the tendency was for a massive spring bloom, followed by either scattered summer flowering, a smaller autumn burst, or sometimes nothing at all until next spring. Due to a limited color palette (white, pink, red) and lack of reliable repeat-bloom, the hybrid perpetuals were ultimately overshadowed by their own descendants, the Hybrid Teas. Examples: 'Ferdinand Pichard', 'Reine Des Violettes', 'Paul Neyron'.

Hybrid Musk

The hybrid musk group was primarily developed by Rev. Joseph Pemberton, a British rosarian, in the first decades of the 20th century, based upon 'Aglaia', a 1896 cross by Peter Lambert. A seedling of this rose, 'Trier', is considered to the be foundation of the class. The genetics of the class are somewhat obscure, as some of the parents are unknown. *Rose multiflora,* however, is known to be one parent, and *R. moschata* (the musk rose) also figures in its heritage, though it is considered to be less important than the name would suggest. Hybrid musks are disease-resistant, remontant and generally cluster-flowered, with a strong, characteristic "musk" scent. Examples include 'Buff Beauty' and 'Penelope'.

Bermuda "Mystery" Roses

The roses have significant value and interest for those growing roses in tropical and semi-tropical regions, since they are highly resistant to both nematode damage and the fungal diseases that plague rose culture in hot, humid areas, and capable of blooming in hot and humid weather. Most of these roses are likely Old Garden Rose cultivars that have otherwise dropped out of cultivation, or sports thereof. They are "mystery roses" because their "proper" historical names have been lost. Tradition dictates that they are named after the owner of the garden where they were rediscovered.

Hybrid Rugosa

Derived from the R. Rugosa species, these vigorous roses are extremely hardy with excellent disease resistance. Most are extremely fragrant, repeat bloomers with moderately double flat flowers. The defining characteristic of a Hybrid Rugosa rose is its wrinkly leaves, but some hybrids do lack this trait. These roses will often set hips. Examples include 'Hansa' and 'Roseraie de l'Häv'.

Miscellaneous

There are also a few smaller classes (such as Scots, Sweet Brier) and some climbing classes of old roses (including Ayrshire, Climbing China, Laevigata, Sempervirens, Boursault, Climbing Tea, and Climbing Bourbon). Those classes with both climbing and shrub forms are often grouped together.

Modern Garden Roses

Classification of modern roses can be quite confusing because many modern roses have old garden roses in their ancestry and their form varies so much. The classifications tend to be by growth and flowering characteristics, such as "large-flowered shrub", "recurrent, large-flowered shrub", "cluster-flowered", "rambler recurrent", or "ground-cover non-recurrent". The following includes the most notable and popular classifications of Modern Garden Roses:

Hybrid Tea

Hybrid teas exhibit traits midway between both parents: hardier than the teas but less hardy than the hybrid perpetuals, and more everblooming than the hybrid perpetuals but less so than the teas. The flowers are well-formed with large, high-centered buds, and each flowering stem typically terminates in a single shapely bloom. The shrubs tend to be stiffly upright and sparsely foliaged, which today is often seen as a liability in the landscape. The hybrid tea class is important in being the first class of roses to include genes from the old Austrian brier rose (*Rosa foetida*). This resulted in an entirely new colour range for roses: shades of deep yellow, apricot, copper, orange, true scarlet, yellow bicolors, lavender, gray, and even brown were now possible. The new color range did much to skyrocket hybrid tea popularity in the 20th century, but these colors came at a price: *Rosa foetida* also passed on a tendency toward disease-susceptibility, scentless blooms, and an intolerance of pruning, to its descendants. Hybrid teas became the single most popular class of garden rose of the 20th century; today, their reputation as being more high maintenance than many other rose classes has led to a decline in hybrid tea popularity among gardeners and landscapers in favor of lower-maintenance "landscape" roses. The hybrid tea remains the standard rose of the floral industry, however, and is still favoured in small gardens in formal situations. Examples: 'Peace', 'Mr. Lincoln,' 'Double Delight.'

Polyantha

Literally "many-flowered" roses, from the Greek "poly" (many) and "anthos" (flower). Originally derived from crosses between two East Asian species (*Rosa chinensis* and *R. multiflora*), polyanthas first appeared in France in the late 1800s alongside the hybrid teas. They featured short plants—some compact, others spreading in habit—with tiny blooms (1" in diameter on average) carried in large sprays, in the typical rose colors of white, pink and red. Their main claim to fame was their prolific bloom: From spring to fall, a healthy polyantha shrub might be literally covered in flowers, creating a strong color impact in the landscape. Polyantha roses are still regarded as low-maintenance, disease-resistant garden roses today, and remain popular for that reason. Examples: 'Cecile Brunner', 'The Fairy', 'Red Fairy'.

Floribunda

Rose breeders quickly saw the value in crossing polyanthas with hybrid teas, to create roses that bloomed with the polyantha profusion, but with hybrid tea floral beauty and color range. In 1909, the first polyantha/hybrid tea cross, 'Gruss an Aachen,' was created, with characteristics midway between both parent classes. As the larger, more shapely flowers and hybrid-tea-like growth habit separated these new roses from polyanthas and hybrid teas alike, a new class was created and named Floribunda, Latin for "many-flowering". Typical floribundas feature stiff shrubs, smaller and bushier than the average hybrid tea but less dense and sprawling than the average polyantha. The flowers are often smaller than hybrid teas but are carried in large sprays, giving a better floral effect in the garden. Floribundas are found in all hybrid tea colors and with the classic hybrid tea-shaped blossom, sometimes differing from hybrid teas only in their cluster-flowering habit. Today they are still used in large bedding schemes in public parks and similar spaces. Examples: 'Dainty Maid', 'Iceberg', 'Tuscan Sun'.

Grandiflora

Grandifloras (Latin for "large-flowered") were the class of roses created in the mid 1900s to designate back-crosses between hybrid teas and floribundas that fit neither category — specifically, the 'Queen Elizabeth' rose, which was introduced in 1954 . Grandiflora shrubs are typically larger than either hybrid teas or floribundas, and feature hybrid tea-style flowers borne in small clusters of three to five, similar to a floribunda. Grandifloras maintained some popularity from about the 1950s to the 1980s but today they are much less popular than either the hybrid teas or the floribundas. Examples: 'Queen Elizabeth', 'Comanche,' 'Montezuma'.

Miniature

All of the classes of Old Garden Roses—gallicas, centifolias, etc.—had corresponding miniature forms, although these were once-flowering just as their larger forms were. As with the standard-sized varieties, miniature Old Garden roses were crossed with repeat-blooming Asian species to produce everblooming miniature roses. Today, miniature roses are represented by twiggy, repeat-flowering shrubs ranging from 6" to 36" in height, with most falling in the 12"–24" height range. Blooms come in all the hybrid tea colours; many varieties also emulate the classic high-centred hybrid tea flower shape. Miniature roses are often marketed and sold by the floral industry as houseplants, but it is important to remember that these plants are largely descended from outdoor shrubs native to temperate regions; thus, most miniature rose varieties require an annual period of cold dormancy to survive. [Examples: *Petite de Hollande* (Miniature Centifolia, once-blooming), *Cupcake* (Modern Miniature, repeat-blooming).]

Climbing/Rambling

As is the case with Miniature roses, all aforementioned classes of roses, both Old and Modern, have "climbing" forms, whereby the canes of the shrubs grow much longer and more flexible than the normal ("bush") forms. In the Old Garden Roses, this is often simply the natural growth habit of many cultivars and varieties; in many Modern roses, however, climbing roses are the results of spontaneous mutations. For example, 'Climbing Peace' is designated as a "Climbing Hybrid Tea," for it is genetically identical to the normal "shrub" form of the 'Peace' hybrid tea rose, except that its canes are long and flexible, i.e. "climbing." Most Climbing roses grow anywhere from 8'–20' in height and exhibit repeat-bloom. Rambler roses, although technically a separate class, are often lumped together with climbing roses. They also exhibit long, flexible canes, but are distinguished from true climbers in two ways: A larger overall size (20'–30' tall is common), and a once-blooming habit. It should be noted that both climbing roses and rambling roses are not true vines such as ivy, clematis or wisteria; they lack the ability to cling to supports on their own, and must be manually trained and tied over structures such as arbors and pergolas. Examples: 'Blaze' (repeat-blooming climber), 'American Pillar' (once-blooming rambler).

English/David Austin

Although not officially recognized as a separate class of roses by any established rose authority, English (aka David Austin) roses are often set aside as such by consumers and retailers alike. Development started in the 1960s by David Austin of Shropshire, England, who wanted to rekindle interest in Old Garden Roses by hybridizing them with modern hybrid teas and floribundas. The idea was to create a new group of roses that featured blooms with old-fashioned shapes and fragrances, evocative of classic gallica, alba and damask roses, but with modern repeat-blooming characteristics and the larger modern color range as well. Austin mostly succeeded in his mission; his tribe of "English" roses, now numbering hundreds of varieties, has been warmly embraced by the gardening public and are widely available to consumers. David Austin roses are still actively developed, with new varieties released regularly. It should be noted that the typical winterhardiness and disease-resistance of the classic Old Garden Roses has largely been compromised in the process; many English roses are susceptible to the same disease problems that plague modern hybrid teas and floribundas, and many are not hardy north of USDA Zone 5. Examples: 'Mary Rose,' 'Graham Thomas', 'Tamora'.

Canadian Hardy Roses

Developed for the extreme weather conditions of Canadian winters, these roses were developed by Agriculture Canada at the Morden Research Station in Morden, Manitoba and the Experimental Farm in Ottawa (and later at L'Assomption, Quebec). These two main lines are called the Parkland series and the Explorer series. These programs have now been discontinued; however the remaining plant stock has been taken over by private breeders via the Canadian Artists series. Derived mostly from crosses of native Canadian species and more tender roses, these plants are extremely tolerant of cold weather, some down to -5°F. A wide diversity of forms and colors were achieved. Examples include 'Morden Belle', 'Winnipeg Parks' and 'Cuthbert Grant'.

Other notable Canadian breeders include Georges Bugnet and Robert Erskine.

Landscape Roses

These are a modern classifation of rose developed mainly for mass amenity planting. In the late 20th century, traditional hybrid tea and floribunda rose varieties fell out of favor amid gardeners and landscapers, as they are often labor- and chemical-intensive plants susceptible to myriad pest and disease problems. So-called "landscape" roses have thus been developed to fill the consumer desire for a garden rose that offers color, form and fragrance, but is also low maintenance and easy to care for. Most landscape roses having the following characteristics:

- Good disease resistance
- Lower growing habit, usually under 60 cm
- Repeat flowering
- Disease and pest resistance
- Non suckering, growing on their own roots.

Principal parties involved in the breeding of new Landscape Roses varieties are Werner Noak (Germany) Meidiland Roses (France) Boot & Co. (Netherlands).

Pruning

Rose pruning, sometimes regarded as a horticultural art form, is largely dependent on the type of rose to be pruned, the reason for pruning, and the time of year it is at the time of the desired pruning.

Most Old Garden Roses of strict European heritage (albas, damasks, gallicas, etc.) are shrubs that bloom once yearly, in late spring or early summer, on two-year-old (or older) canes. As such, their pruning requirements are quite minimal, and are overall similar to any other analogous shrub, such as lilac or forsythia. Generally, only old, spindly canes should be pruned away, to make room for new canes. One -year-old canes should never be pruned because doing so will remove next year's flower buds. The shrubs can also be pruned back lightly, immediately after the blooms fade, to reduce the overall height or width of the plant. In general, pruning requirements for OGRs are much less laborious and regimented than for Modern hybrids.

Modern hybrids, including the hybrid teas, floribundas, grandifloras, modern miniatures, and English roses, have a complex genetic background that almost always includes China roses (*R. chinensis*). China roses were evergrowing, everblooming roses from humid subtropical regions that bloomed constantly on any new vegetative growth produced during the growing season. Their modern hybrid descendants exhibit similar habits: Unlike Old Garden Roses, modern hybrids bloom continuously (until stopped by frost) on any new canes produced during the growing season. They therefore require pruning away of any spent flowering stem, in order to divert the plant's energy into producing new growth and thence new flowers.

Additionally, Modern Hybrids planted in cold-winter climates will almost universally require a "hard" annual pruning (reducing all canes to 8"–12" in height) in early spring. Again, because of their complex China rose background, Modern Hybrids are typically not as cold-hardy as European OGRs, and low winter temperatures often desiccate or kill exposed canes. In spring, if left unpruned, these damanged canes will often die back all the way to the shrub's root zone, resulting in a weakened, disfigured plant. The annual "hard" pruning of hybrid teas, floribundas, etc. should generally be done in early spring; most gardeners coincide this pruning with the blooming of forsythia shrubs. Canes should be cut about 1/2" above a vegetative bud (identifiable as a point on a cane where a leaf once grew).

For both Old Garden Roses and Modern Hybrids, any weak, damaged or diseased growth should be pruned away completely, regardless of the time of year. Any pruning of any rose should also be done so that the cut is made at a forty five degree angle above a vegetative bud. This helps the pruned stem callus over more quickly, and also mitigates moisture buildup over the cut, which can lead to disease problems.

For all general rose pruning (including cutting flowers for arrangements), sharp secateurs (hand-held, sickle-bladed pruners) should be used to cut any growth 1/2" or less in diameter. For canes of a thickness greater than 1/2", pole loppers or a small handsaw are generally more effective; secateurs may be damaged or broken in such instances.

Deadheading

Deadheading is the simple practice of manually removing any spent, faded, withered, or discoloured flowers from rose shrubs over the course of the blooming season. The purpose of deadheading is to encourage the plant to focus its energy and resources on forming new offshoots and blooms, rather than in fruit production. Deadheading may also be performed, if spent flowers are unsightly, for aethestic purposes. Roses are particularly responsive to deadheading.

Deadheading causes different effects on different varieties of roses. For continual blooming varieties, whether Old Garden roses or more modern hybrid varieties, deadheading allows the rose plant to continue forming new shoots, leaves, and blooms. For "once-blooming" varieties (that bloom only once each season), deadheading has the effect of causing the plant to form new green growth, even though new blooms will not form until the next blooming season. For most rose gardeners, deadheading is used to refresh the growth of the rose plants to keep the rose plants strong, vibrant, and productive.

The rose has always been valued for its beauty and has a long history of symbolism. The ancient Greeks and Romans identified the rose with their goddesses of love referred to as Aphrodite and Venus. In Rome a wild rose would be placed on the door of a room where secret or confidential matters were discussed. The phrase *sub rosa*, or "under the rose", means to keep a secret — derived from this ancient Roman practice. Early Christians identified the five petals of the rose with the five wounds of Christ. Despite this interpretation, their leaders were hesitant to adopt it because of its association with Roman excesses and pagan ritual. The red rose was eventually adopted as a symbol of the blood of the Christian martyrs. Roses also later came to be associated with the Virgin Mary.

Rose culture came into its own in Europe in the 1800s with the introduction of perpetual blooming roses from China. There are currently thousands of varieties of roses developed for bloom shape, size, fragrance and even for lack of prickles. Popular culture.

A Red Rose

Roses are ancient symbols of love and beauty. The rose was sacred to a number of goddesses (including Isis and Aphrodite), and is often used as a symbol of the Virgin Mary. 'Rose' means pink or red in a variety of languages (such as Romance languages, Greek, and Polish).

The rose is the national flower of England and the United States, as well as being the symbol of England Rugby, and of the Rugby Football Union. It is also the provincial flower of Yorkshire and Lancashire in England (the white rose and red rose respectively) and of Alberta (the wild rose), and the state flower of four US states: Iowa and North Dakota (*R. arkansana*), Georgia (*R. laevigata*), and New York] (*Rosa* generally). Portland, Oregon counts "City of Roses" among its nicknames, and holds an annual Rose Festival.

Roses are occasionally the basis of design for rose windows, such windows comprising five or ten segments (the five petals and five sepals of a rose) or multiples thereof; however most Gothic rose windows are much more elaborate and were probably based originally on the wheel and other symbolism.

A red rose (often held in a hand) is a symbol of socialism or social democracy; it is also used as a symbol by the British and Irish Labour Parties, as well as by the French, Spanish (Spanish Socialist Workers' Party), Portuguese, Norwegian, Danish, Swedish, Finnish, Brazilian, Dutch (Partij van de Arbeid) and European socialist or social democratic parties. This originated when the red rose was used as a badge by the marchers in the May 1968 street protests in Paris. White Rose was a World War II non violent resistance group in Germany.

Quotes

- *What's in a name? That which we call a rose/By any other name would smell as sweet.* — William Shakespeare, Romeo and Juliet act II, sc. ii.
- *O, my love's like a red, red rose/That's newly sprung in June* — Robert Burns, A Red, Red Rose.
- *Information appears to stew out of me naturally, like the precious ottar of roses out of the otter.* Mark Twain, Roughing it.
- *Hearts starve as well as bodies; give us bread, but give us roses.* — James Oppenheim, "Bread and Roses".
- *Rose is a rose is a rose is a rose* — Gertrude Stein, *Sacred Emily* (1913), a poem included in *Geography and Plays.*

Perfume : Rose oil

Rose perfumes are made from attar of roses or rose oil, which is a mixture of volatile essential oils obtained by steam distilling the crushed petals of roses. The technique originated in Persia (the word Rose itself is from Persian) then spread through Arabia and India, but nowadays about 70% to 80% of production is in the Rose Valley near Kazanluk in Bulgaria, with some production in Qamsar in Iran and Germany. The Kaaba in Mecca is annually washed by the Iranian rose water from Qamsar. In Bulgaria, Iran and Germany, damask roses (*Rosa damascena* 'Trigintipetala') are used. In the French rose oil industry *Rosa centifolia* is used. The oil, pale yellow or yellow-grey in color, is sometimes called 'Rose Absolute' oil to distinguish it from diluted versions. The weight of oil extracted is about one three-thousandth to one six-thousandth of the weight of the flowers; for example, about two thousand flowers are required to produce one gram of oil.

The main constituents of attar of roses are the fragrant alcohols geraniol and l-citronellol; and rose camphor, an odourless paraffin. ß-Damascenone is also a significant contributor to the scent.

9

Improve Yield with High Quality Seed

Introduction

- Seeds are one of the least expensive but most important factors influencing yield potential.
- Seed quality is determined by germination and purity analysis.
- By law, all crop seeds must be labeled for germination percent, crop seed, weed seed and inert matter content, and the date of germination test.
- Purchase seed stock from a reputable seed dealer who has proper cleaning, handling and storage facilities.

Seeds are one of the least expensive but most important factors influencing yield potential. Crop seeds contain all the genetic information to determine yield potential, adaptation to environmental conditions, and resistance to insect pests and disease.

One of a farmer's most critical management decisions is the selection of seed source and variety. The cost of seed stocks usually is less than 5 to 10 per cent of total production costs. Yet seed stocks can affect the yield potential of a crop more than any other input factor.

Seed Quality

Seed quality is determined by many factors, principally seed purity and germination. However, many other factors, such as the variety, presence of seed-borne disease, vigor of the seed, and seed size are important when considering seed purchase.

Seed purity is determined by the amount of unwanted material present in the pure seed. Contaminants such as noxious weed seed, unwanted crop seed or inert matter not only increase production costs, but also substantially reduce the quality and quantity of the harvest. If you purchase seed that has not been properly conditioned to remove unwanted weed seed, include in your decision-making the increased herbicide cost to control newly introduced noxious or common weeds.

Seed germination tests assess the ability of the seed to produce a healthy plant when placed under favorable environmental conditions. Germination tests are conducted for a prescribed time period under laboratory conditions that assure optimum moisture, temperature and light. Unfortunately, these conditions are seldom encountered in the field, and field emergence may be overestimated by standard germination tests.

Seed lots that have low germination also are less vigorous due to seed deterioration. As seeds deteriorate, loss of vigour precedes loss of viability, so seeds with low germination usually will be less vigorous. Hence, in seed lots with poor germination, those seeds that do germinate often produce weaker seedlings with reduced yield potential. However, some species (such as many native grasses) have inherently low germination potential and cannot be assumed to have poor vigor due to low germination.

Varietal purity indicates genetic purity of the seed. This factor is extremely important in obtaining pure stands of a specific variety. Varietal mixtures can cause uneven maturity, lower yield potential, increased susceptibility to disease and insect pests, and be less adapted to specific environmental conditions.

Varietal mixtures are difficult to detect through examination of the physical characteristics of the seed. Seed certification programmes and many seed companies rely heavily on inspection of the seed production field to assure varietal purity. When choosing seed stocks, select those that are labeled by variety name, preferably certified seed. When you purchase certified seed, obtain proper documentation to prove that the seed has been certified, such as a certified seed tag or bulk sales certificate that shows the variety by name.

Seed vigour usually cannot be assessed by the Consumer. Germination and seed size (in the case of cereal grains) often are good indicators of seed vigor. However, in the case of hybrid varieties, seed size or plumpness is sometimes not related to seed vigor. Research in Kansas and other states shows significant yield increases when large seeds were compared to small seeds from the same lot. These differences were accentuated when deep planting was used and point out the need to remove the small seed during seed conditioning.

Seed Labeling

State and federal laws require that all agricultural seed be labeled. Labeling requirements for some flower, tree and shrub seeds may differ. If the seed has been treated a label must state the seed has been treated, the commonly accepted coined chemical name of the applied substance, and if the substance in the amount present is harmful to human or other vertebrate animals, a caution statement such as "Do not use for food, feed, or oil purposes." Toxic substances shall be labeled with a poison symbol. Terms that must appear on the label are:

- varietal name and kind of seed;
- lot number;
- percentage by weight of pure seed;
- percentage by weight of all weed seeds;
- percentage by weight of all crop seeds;
- percentage by weight of inert matter;

- name and number per pound of restricted noxious weed seeds; and
- the date of the germination test.

Terms that appear on the label are:

Variety name: The name of the kind or kind and variety for each agricultural seed component present in excess of 5 percent of the whole and the percentage by weight of each. If the variety is not stated, the label shall show the kind and the words "Variety Not Stated" or "VNS". Hybrids shall be labeled as hybrids.

Lot Number: A lot number or other lot identification.

Origin: State or foreign country of origin if known; if not known, the fact shall be stated.

Pure seed: The percentage by weight of crop seed compared to other components. The best quality seed is nearly 100 percent pure. To meet certified seed standards for small grains, seed must be more than 98 percent pure.

Other crop seed: The percentage by weight of any other crop seed in the test sample.

Inert matter: The percentage by weight of sand, sticks, broken seed parts and other foreign material in the seed. This percentage is small in high-quality seed. Higher percentages of inert material will increase the cost of the remaining pure, live seed.

Weed seed content: The percentage by weight of weed seed. State seed regulations do not allow any prohibited noxious weed seeds to be present. Any restricted noxious weed seed content **must** be listed on the label.

Germination: The percentage of germination, exclusive of hard or dormant seed. The percentage of dormant or hard seed if present and the calendar month and year the germination test was completed. The date of test should be within the previous 13 months on the time of sale to ensure the quality of seed and to comply with seed laws.

Labeler: The name and address of the person who labeled the seed.

Purchasing Quality Seed Stock

High quality seed can be purchased from any reputable seed dealer who has experience in producing, conditioning (cleaning) and storing seed stocks.

During seed production, proper fertilization, adequate water, sufficient isolation (for cross pollinated crops), proper roguing of off-types, and timely harvests are all important factors. Care also must be taken to clean harvesting equipment, trucks, and storage and handling facilities to prevent contamination. During the conditioning and packaging process, the seed must be handled carefully to avoid contamination and damage.

Proper seed moisture at the time of packaging and seed treatment also are important considerations. Seed storage conditions must maintain the vigor and quality of the seed. Excess humidity or heat can cause severe damage to seed in a short time.

Seed dealers should have the capability and facilities to provide the conditions listed above. Their reputation as quality seed dealers usually is a good indicator of the quality of seed offered for sale. Don't hesitate to ask questions regarding the origin of the seed and appearance of the seed field. If the dealer is a neighbor, ask to see the seed production fields prior to harvest.

10

Regulatory Regimen for Genetically Modified Foods

INTRODUCTION

During recent years there has been considerable advancement of Science andTechnology for using Modern Biotechnology tools for the production of foods, feeds anddrugs. These include the cultivation of genetically modified (GM) crops, use of genetically modified organisms (GMO), specially recombinant bacteria and developmentof transgenic animal models especially using dairy cattle as bioreactors for producing pharmaceuticals to alter composition of cows milk to resemble human milk. Research is also helping in developing plants such as banana with vaccine against cholera and tomato and muskmelon with vaccine against rabies. Cures even for diabetes and cancer have been attempted with encouraging results through the production of immune proteins in plants. However, among these global developments, the cultivation of GM crops developed for both food and industrial purposes are most important in the Indian context.

In the year 2003 genetically modified crops were cultivated in 67.7 million hectares (167 million acres) which involved 7 million farmers in 18 countries. There has been a 40-fold increase in the global area of transgenic crops form 1996 to 2003. Around

20 million hectares in developing countries were used for GM crops. The following six countries grew 99% of the global transgenic crops: Country Area in million hectares (%) of Global total USA 42.8 (63), Argentina 13.9 (21), Canada 4.4 (6), Brazil 3.0 (44), China 2.8 (4), South Africa 0.4 (1). The rest of the countries like Australia, Mexico, India and EU countries like Spain, France and Germany, contribute remaining one per cent. India grew *Bt* cotton in around 0.1 million hectares in 2003 which was double of 2002. Brazil and Philippines initiated planting of GM crops (herbicide tolerant soybean and *Bt* maize respectively) in 2003.

The genetically engineered crops (GEC) commercially cultivated include cotton, soyabean, maize, canola, tomatoes, potatoes and squash. Among these, four crops dominate the GMO markets of the world with soyabean being the most important (61%-41.4 million hectares), followed by maize (23%-15.5 million hectares), cotton (11%-7.2 million hectares) and canola (5%-3.6 milllion hectares). The rest of the crops constituted 0.1% of the total acreage under GM crops. Seventy-three per cent of the GM crops raised were for herbicide tolerance, 18% were aimed at resistance to insects and 8% were varieties containing both traits. Only less than 0.1% of the crop was aimed at other characteristics like yield improvement, vitamin enrichment, etc. Although the cultivation of GM crops have been claimed to be profitable to farmers, the impact varies by year, location, crop, etc. The global market in transgenic plants is estimated to grow rapidly to $6 billion by the year 2005.

From the Indian view point, more than herbicide resistance, stress resistance to drought, temperature and poor soils, nutritional enrichment, increased productivity and pest resistance are important. Also GM varieties which will eliminate the problem of naturally occurring toxins like the unusual toxic amino acid in *Lathyrus sativus* areimportant for us.

Concerns

Although GM plants have the potential to improve agriculture production, food quality, nutrition and health, various uncertainties exist regarding safety of these foods because there is limited scientific evidence regarding their toxicity or health risks, themethodology used for assessing the risks is not robust enough or sensitive enough, and the molecular and genetic effects of the technology are unpredictable in nature. Widespread concerns have been expressed by the public and scientists about effect of GM foods on the environment, lack of consumer benefits, ethical issues and the perception that a few large multinational corporations will be the prime beneficiaries andwould dictate world markets.

Emergence of Resistance

Many crops have been engineered for pest disease andherbicide resistance. There could be a potential for development of resistance in thetarget organism. This has been particularly observed in crops developed for insectresistance like cotton. This has resulted in the use of a 'refugia' while cultivating *Bt*crops. Similarly in the case of herbicide resistance crops like soyabean, a potential for development of superweeds due to spread of herbicide resistance from GM crops to weeds exists.

Genetic Pollution and Pollen Movement

The potential for transfer of pollen from GM crops to other plant species has been an issue of much concern. For example, the transgenic material from a GM maize cultivated by a farmer can be transferred without 6 the farmer's knowledge to a non-GM maize cultivated in the neighbouring field. Such kind of pollen transfer varies with different environmental conditions.

Loss of Biodiversity

Contamination of non-GM varieties of plants through pollen driftcan cause loss of biodiversity.

Health and Safety Concerns

The use of recombinant DNA (rDNA) technology in the production of GM foods involves transfer of genes from different species into the food producing organism. Such a transfer is facilitated along with various regulatory elements obtained from bacterial or viral sources that are required to empower to produce the trait in the host organism. The safety of these components of the genetic construct is not clearly known as they have the potential to induce toxicity, transfer to gut flora or produce unintended effects leading to changes that are relevant from toxicological/nutritional perspective. Specific safety issues associated with GM foods include direct or indirect consequences of new gene product or altered levels of existing gene product due to GM, possibility of gene transfer from ingested GM food and potential adverse effect like allergenicity and toxic effects.

Depending on the modified component, the GM food may contain or consist of GMO or be produced from GMO but not contain GMO. The safety concerns are centered aroundpotential toxicological and nutritional changes that could be harmful to human health.

Toxicity Potential

Various toxicants are known to be inherently present in different plants. Genetic engineering has the potential to alter such constituents or produce newer toxicants. Crops developed for pest resistance and herbicide resistance are particularly focused for toxicity concern. The case of GM potatoes experiencing *Galanthus nivalis* lectin gene for insecticidal properties is an example of the potential of GM foods to cause toxicity. In a group of rats fed with GM potato damage to immune systems and stunted growth was observed and the experiment had generated considerable controversy.

Nutritional Composition

Genetic modification of plants may result in alteration in nutritional composition which in turn may affect the nutritional status of the consumer or population groups. Currently developed plants with improved nutritive value include GM rice with enriched vitamin A and GM soyabean and rapeseed with modified fatty acid. The impact of such intended modification in nutrient level in crop plants can affect nutritional status of the individual. There is also the potential for unexpected alteration in nutrients as it was observed in the case of GM rice (accumulation of xanthophylls, increase in prolamines). Such changes can affect nutrient profiles resulting in nutritional imbalances in the consumer.

Allergenicity

The allergenicity potential of the new protein expressed on the transgene inserted into the plant is a major food safety concern. Most traits introduced into GM crops result from the expression of one or more protein that may possess allergenic properties. Crops modified for insect resistance have been shown to have the potential for allergic responses. This has been highlighted in the recent findings of Starlink variety of GM maize which has been shown to possess allergic properties in the food chain in USA, EU and Japan. The allergenicity potential of GM food has often been difficult to establish with existing methods as the transgenes transferred are frequently from sources not eaten before, many have unknown allergenicity or there may be a potential for genetic modification process to result in increase of an allergen already present in the food.

Antibiotic Resistance-Potential for Gene transfer

Concern has been expressed on the possibility of transfer of GM DNA from the plant to gut microflora of humans and animals. Of importance have been the antibiotic resistant genes that are frequently used as selection markers, in the genetic modification process. Such genes have the potential to adversely affect the therapeutic efficacy of orally administered antibiotics. It is significant to point out that there has been no report of any adverse health effects of GM foods and there are no peer reviewed publications on the healtheffects of GM foods in humans. Many persons feel that gene transplantation processes to the germ plasm of crops violates the natural order, but it is not clear how this technique of genetic modification is distinct from plant hybridization, chemically or radioactively induced mutations, cell fusions or synthetic foods? Concerns have also been raised by vegetarian groups on using animal genes in plants.

Socioeconomic Concerns

The perspective on the use of modern biotechnology for food and agriculture differs not only among the developed countries and developing countries but also differs among high income countries. While most EU countries are not enthusiastic about GM food, it is more acceptable for countries like Australia,

Canada and USA because of the importance of export of agriculture to their countries. Developing countries such as Argentina and China are promoting GM foods in a big way. Some developing countries considering commercialization of GM crops are hesitant to do so because of the fear of losing access to the European market not only for commodities that have been genetically nine modified but also for those that have not been modified. Practically it would be difficult to keep GM and non-GM commodities separate and often they could get mixed.

Modern agriculture biotechnology is increasingly subjected to Intellectual Property protection, and is generally developed by Private Sector companies. This could also lead to reduced competition, monopoly of profits and exploitation of small farmers. It is also felt that GM crop production may harm small farmers in the developing countries as imported GM commodities will undercut local production. Agriculture biotechnology could lead to increased inequality of income and wealth because large farmers may capture most of the benefits. The potential benefits could include the productivity gains needed to feed the increasing population, lesser expenditure on pesticides/herbicides, improved nutritive value, durability of products during post harvest stage, etc.

Current Status of Safety Assessment of GM Foods-International

The safety assessment of GM food has been addressed by several international organizations like the Organization for Economic Cooperation and Development (OECD), Food and Agriculture Organization (FAO), World Health Organization (WHO) and Codex Alimentarius Commission (CAC). The general consensus of these organizations has been that the safety assessment of GM foods requires an integrated andstepwise case-by-case approach. Various strategies have been designed to assess thesafety of GM crops and these have been evaluated in a series of workshops and meetings.

Joint FAO/WHO Expert Consultations on Foods Derived from Biotechnology

Various consultations have been convened by WHO and FAO to address the safety issuesconcerning GM foods. The concept of Substantial Equivalence (SE), initially formulated by OECD and evaluated in these consultations, became a key element in the safetyassessment procedures for GM foods. Substantial Equivalence involves a comparativeapproach where the relative safety of GM food or food component to an existing food or food component is established. Factors taken into account in the safety assessmentinclude phenotypic, agronomic and functional characteristics as well as potential intakeand dietary impact of the introduction of GM foods. The outcome of such comparison will be that the food is: (i) SE and thus no further testing is required; (ii) SE except for the inserted trait such that the focus of safety testing is on this trait or; (iii) not SE and a caseby- case assessment is carried out according to the characteristics of the new product.

Depending on the type of outcome the food is subjected to further nutritional and toxicological studies. A decision-tree approach has also been prepared by some authorities for determining the extent of testing required in specific cases. The SE determinations have been carried out for a variety of GM crops.

Codex Alimentarius Commission

The Codex Alimentarius Commission of the FAO/WHO set up an Ad-hoc intergovernmental task force on foods derived from biotechnology to develop standards, guidelines and recommendations for foods derived from biotechnology. The task force identified that the risk assessment of GM foods requires scientific data which addresses the current safety concerns of GM foods like the effect of the genetic modification process including the function and properties of newly inserted genes, the safety and nutritional properties of newly expressed substances in the food and their impact on diet, potential for allergenicity, potential for gene transfer to human and animal cells, and unexpected changes in the composition of the modified product due to insertion of novel 11 genes or suppression of constituent genes. A draft guideline for the conduct of safety assessment of foods derived from genetically modified plants has been brought out by thetask force.

Cartagena Protocol on Biosafety

The Cartagena Protocol was negotiated under the auspices of the Convention of Biological Diversity (CBD) in 1992. The Protocol provides rules for safe transfer, handling and disposal of Living Modified Organisms (LMOs) or Genetically Modified Organisms (GMOs). Its aim is to address the threats posed by LMOs to biological diversity, also taking into account the risks to human health. The Protocol takes into account the general principles of risk assessment developed by international bodies. Two features of the protocol, the Advance Information Agreement (AIA) and the Precautionary Approach are being incorporated in risk/safety assessment procedures in many countries particularly in the context of trade in GMOs. The AIA provides for a prior assessment by importing country of GMOs intentionally introduced into the environment like seeds for plantation, live fish for release etc. This agreement calls for documentation and identification of LMOs which include the relevant trait, information handling, storage, transport and use along with a full report or risk assessment. In making the decision to import, the Protocol allows a precautionary approach to be used to restrict or ban the GMO if there is a lack of scientific certainty due to insufficient information on the potential risks that LMOs can have on biodiversity and human health.

World Trade Organization (WTO) Agreements

The WTO is mainly involved in establishing rules for international trade in GM foods. Two agreements in the WTO apply to risk assessment and labeling of GM foods. These are the Agreements on Sanitary and Phytosanitary Measures (SPS) and Technical Barriers to Trade (TBT). The risk assessment of GM foods for trade requirements is addressed under the agreement on Sanitary and Phytosanitary Measures (SPS). This agreement deals with application of food safety and animal and plant health regulations. By imposing science-based disciplines and requiring risk assessment based on science and applied only to the extent necessary to protect human, animal or plant life or health, it aims to prevent governments from using health and safety laws to limit international trade. The TBT agreement assists to ensure that WTO members do not use domestic regulations, standards, testing and certification procedures to create unnecessary obstacles to trade. It encourages countries to use international standards where appropriate.

Regulatory System for GM foods in Selected Countries USA

Regulation: Coordinated framework for regulation in biotechnology.

Agency for environmental safety assessment: USDA, EPA

Agency for food safety evaluation: FDA.

Highlights

— Sectoral approach regulation

— Procedures for notification, performance standards, safety standards.

— Labeling policies: no mandatory labeling.

— Mandatory pre-market approval (under consideration).

European Union (EU)

Regulation: Environmental release and marketing, contained use, safety review and labeling. Agency: Directives for deliberate release into environment and placing on the market.

Highlights

— Procedures for authorization and notification.

— Procedures for risk assessment.

— Mandatory monitoring, labeling and traceability, consultation of scientific committees, consultation of public - Establishment of one per cent threshold for adventitious contamination of non-GM with GMO.

Australia

Regulation: National Gene Technology Regulatory System.

Agency: Office of the Gene Technology Regulatory.

Highlights:

— Whole of government approach - Labeling of foods containing GM protein or DNA in final product - Minor ingredients and highly refined oils exempt from labelling - one per cent tolerance for unintended mixture.

China

Agency: Safety Administration Office for Agricultural Biological Genetic Engineering(Ministry of Agriculture).

Highlights:

— Procedure for administration of registration of imported feed and food additives-Labeling requirements for all imported GM soyabean, corn, rapeseed, cottonseed and tomatoes-Approval procedure for release into environment.

Current Regulatory System in India

The following are the existing guidelines in India for transgenic crops:

A. The EPA Act, 1986 and Rules, 1989 of Ministry of Environment and Forests, namely which deals with rules and procedures for handling GMOs and hazardous organisms. The Genetic Engineering Approval Committee (GEAC) established by the Ministry acts as a statutory body for review and approval from environmental angle of activities involving large scale use of GMOs and their products in R&D, industrial production, environmental release and field application. The Ministries of Environment and Forests has issued a draft notification in July 2001 as an amendment regarding the permission and approval of foodstuffs. This notification restricts a person from importing, manufacture transport, store, distribute or sale of any food, feed, raw or processed or any ingredient of food, food additives or any food product that contains GM material,without the approval of the GEAC. A Biotechnology Coordination Committeeunder the GEAC functions as the legal and statutory body with judicial powers to inspect, investigate and take punitive action in case of violation of statutory provision under EPA. Issues for action include review and control, and monitoring of large scale use of GMOs in R&D and industrial production, environmental release and experimental field trials.

B. The Review Committee on Genetic Manipulation (RCGM) under the Department of Biotechnology (DBT), Ministry of Science and Technology, monitors the safety related aspects of ongoing research projects involving GMOs. It brings out manuals of guidelines specifying procedures for regulatory process, activities involving GMOs in research, use and application from environmental safety angle (Recombinant DNA Safety Guidelines 1992 and Revised Guidelines for Research in Transgenic Plants 1998). The mechanism of implementation of guidelines is through the Recombinant DNA Advisory Committee (RDAC) and Institutional Biosafety Committee (IBSC). The RDAC takes note of development at national and international levels in biotechnology on recombinant research, use and application while the IBSC is the nodal point for interaction within an Institute, University, Commercial Organization included in rDNA research or implementation of rDNA guidelines. The IBSC is constituted in all centres engaged in genetic engineering research and production activities. Such committee should also include a representative from the health sector. In addition there is a provision of State Biotechnology Coordination Committee (SBCC) and District LevelCommittee (DLC).

11

Plant Science or Phytology

INTRODUCTION

Plant science(s) or phytology, or plant biology is a branch of biology and is the scientific study of plant life and development. Botany covers a wide range of scientific disciplines that study plants, algae, and fungi including: structure, growth, reproduction, metabolism, development, diseases, and chemical properties and evolutionary relationships between the different groups. Botany, the study of plants, began with tribal efforts to identify edible, medicinal and poisonous plants, making botany one of the oldest sciences. From this ancient interest in plants, the scope of botany has increased to include the study of over 550,000 kinds or species of living organisms.

Hibiscus

As with other life forms in biology, plant life can be studied from different perspectives, from the molecular, genetic and biochemical level through organelles, cells, tissues, organs, individuals, plant populations, and communities of plants. At each of these levels a botanist might be concerned with the classification (taxonomy), structure (anatomy and morphology), or function (physiology) of plant life.

Historically all living things were grouped as animals or plants, and botany covered all organisms not considered animals.

Some organisms once included in the field of botany are no longer considered to belong to the plant kingdom — these include fungi (studied in mycology), lichens (lichenology), bacteria (bacteriology), viruses (virology) and single-celled algae, which are now grouped as part of the Protista. However, attention is still given to these groups by botanists, and fungi, lichens, bacteria and photosynthetic protists are usually covered in introductory botany courses.

The study of plants is vital because they are a fundamental part of life on earth, which generates the oxygen, food, fibres, fuel and medicine that allow humans and other higher life forms to exist. Through photosynthesis, plants also absorb carbon dioxide, a greenhouse gas that in large amounts can affect global climate, they prevent soil erosion and impact the water cycle. Paleobotanists study ancient plants in the fossil record. It is believed that early in the earth's history, the evolution of photosynthetic plants altered the global atmosphere of the earth, changing the ancient atmosphere by oxidation. A good understanding of plants is crucial to the future of human societies as it allows us to:

- Produce food to feed an expanding population
- Understand fundamental life processes
- Produce medicine and materials to treat diseases and other ailments
- Understand environmental changes more clearly

Human Nutrition

Virtually all foods eaten come from plants, either directly from staple foods and other fruit and vegetables, or indirectly through livestock or other animals, which rely on plants for their nutrition. Plants are the fundamental base of nearly all food chains because they use the energy from the sun and nutrients from the soil and atmosphere and convert them into a form that can be consumed and utilized by animals; this is what ecologists call the first trophic level. Botanists also study how plants produce food we can eat and how to increase yields and therefore their work is important in mankind's ability to *feed the world* and provide food security for future generations, for example through plant breeding. Botanists also study weeds, plants which are considered to be a nuisance in a particular location. Weeds are a considerable problem in agriculture, and botany provides some of the basic science used to understand how to minimize 'weed' impact in agriculture and native ecosystems. Ethnobotany is the study of the relationships between plants and people.

Gregor Mendel laid the foundations of modern genetics from his studies of plants.

Fundamental Life Processes

Plants are convenient organisms in which fundamental life processes (like cell division and protein synthesis for example) can be studied, without the ethical dilemmas of studying animals or humans. The genetic laws of inheritance were discovered in this way by Gregor Mendel, who was studying the way pea shape is inherited. What Mendel learned from studying plants has had far reaching benefits outside of botany. Additionally, Barbara McClintock discovered 'jumping genes' by studying maize. These are a few examples that demonstrate how botanical research has an ongoing relevance to the understanding of fundamental biological processes.

Medicine and Materials

Many medicinal and recreational drugs, such as tetrahydrocannabinol, caffeine, and nicotine come directly from the plant kingdom. Others are simple derivatives of botanical natural products; for example aspirin is based on the pain killer salicylic acid which originally came from the bark of willow trees. There may be many novel cures for diseases provided by plants, waiting to be discovered. Popular stimulants such as coffee, chocolate, tobacco, and tea also come from plants. Most alcoholic beverages come from fermenting plants such as barley (beer), rice (*saki*) and grapes (wine).

Plants also provide us with many natural materials, such as cotton, wood, paper, linen, vegetable oils, some types of rope, and rubber. The production of silk would not be possible without the cultivation of the mulberry plant. Sugarcane, rapeseed, soy and other plants with a highly-fermentable sugar or oil content have recently been put to use as sources of biofuels, which are important alternatives to fossil fuels, see biodiesel.

Environmental Changes

Plants can also help us understand changes in on our environment in many ways, i.e.:

- Understanding habitat destruction and species extinction is dependent on an accurate and complete catalog of plant systematics and taxonomy.
- Plant responses to ultraviolet radiation can help us monitor problems like the ozone depletion.
- Analyzing pollen deposited by plants thousands or millions of years ago can help scientists to reconstruct past climates and predict future ones, an essential part of climate change research.
- Recording and analyzing the timing of plant life cycles are important parts of phenology used in climate-change research.
- Lichens, which are sensitive to atmospheric conditions, have been extensively used as pollution indicators.

In many different ways, plants can act a little like the 'miners canary', an *early warning system* alerting us to important changes in our environment. In addition to these practical and scientific reasons, plants are extremely valuable as recreation for millions of people who enjoy gardening, horticultural and culinary uses of plants every day.

Early Botany

Early examples of plant taxonomy occur in the Rigveda, that divides plants into *V?ska* (tree), *Osadhi* (herbs useful to humans) and *Virudha* (creepers). which are further subdivided. The *Atharvaveda* divides plants into eight classes, *Visakha* (spreading branches), *Manjari* (leaves with long clusters), *Sthambini* (bushy plants), *Prastanavati* (which expands); *Ekasrnga* (those with monopodial growth), *Pratanavati* (creeping plants), *Amsumati* (with many stalks), and *Kandini* (plants with knotty joints). The *Taittiriya Samhita* and classifies the plant kingdom into *vrksa, vana* and *druma* (trees), *visakha* (shrubs with spreading branches), *sasa* (herbs), *amsumali* (a spreading or deliquescent plant), *vratati* (climber), *stambini* (bushy plant), *pratanavati* (creeper), and *alasala* (those spreading on the ground). *Manusmriti* proposed a classification of plants in eight major categories. Charaka Samhita and Sushruta Samhita and the Vaisesikas also present an elaborate taxonomy. *Parashara*, the author of *Vrksayurveda* (the science of life of trees), classifies plants into *Dvimatrka* (Dicotyledons) and *Ekamatrka* (Monocotyledons). These are further classified into *Samiganiya* (Fabaceae), *Puplikagalniya* (Rutaceae), *Svastikaganiya* (Cruciferae), *Tripuspaganiya* (Cucurbitaceae), *Mallikaganiya* (Apocynaceae), and *Kurcapuspaganiya* (Asteraceae). Other important medieval Indian works of plant physiology include the *Prthviniraparyam* of Udayana, *Nyayavindutika* of Dharmottara, *Saddarsana-samuccaya* of Gunaratna, and *Upaskara* of Sankaramisra.

Ancient China

In ancient China, the recorded listing of different plants and herb concoctions for pharmaceutical purposes spans back to at least the Warring States (481 BC-221 BC). Many Chinese writers over the centuries contributed to the written knowledge of herbal pharmaceutics. There was the Han Dynasty (202 BC-AD 220) written work of the Huangdi Neijing and the famous pharmacologist Zhang Zhongjing of the 2nd century. There was also the 11th century scientists and statesmen Su Song and Shen Kuo, who compiled treatises on herbal medicine and included the use of mineralogy.

Greco-Roman World

Among the earliest of botanical works in Europe, written around 300 B.C., are two large treatises by Theophrastus: *On the History of Plants* (*Historia Plantarum*) and *On the Causes of Plants*. Together these books constitute the most important contribution to botanical science during antiquity and on into the Middle Ages. The Roman medical writer Dioscorides provides important evidence on Greek and Roman knowledge of medicinal plants.

Medieval Botany

The Kurdish biologist Al-Dinawari (828-896) is considered the founder of Arabic botany for his *Book of Plants*, in which he described at least 637 plants and discussed plant evolution from its birth to its death, describing the phases of plant growth and the production of flowers and fruit.

In the early 13th century, the Andalusian-Arabian biologist Abu al-Abbas al-Nabati developed an early scientific method for botany, introducing empirical and experimental techniques in the testing, description and identification of numerous materia medica, and separating unverified reports from those supported by actual tests and observations. His student Ibn al-Baitar (d. 1248) wrote a pharmaceutical encyclopedia describing 1,400 plants, foods, and drugs, 300 of which were his own original discoveries. A Latin translation of his work was useful to European biologists and pharmacists in the 18th and 19th centuries.

Early Modern Botany

In 1665, using an early microscope, Robert Hooke discovered cells in cork, and a short time later in living plant tissue. The German Leonhart Fuchs, the Swiss Conrad von Gesner, and the British authors Nicholas Culpeper and John Gerard published herbals that gave information on the medicinal uses of plants.

During the 18th century systems of classification became deliberately artificial and served only for the purpose of identification. These classifications are comparable to diagnostic keys, where taxa are artificially grouped in pairs by few, easily recognisable characters. The sequence of the taxa in keys is often totally unrelated to their natural or phyletic groupings. In the 18th century an increasing number of new plants had arrived in Europe, from newly discovered countries and the European colonies worldwide, and a larger amount of plants became available for study.

In 1754 Carl von Linné (Carl Linnaeus) divided the plant Kingdom into 25 classes. One, the *Cryptogamia*, included all the plants with concealed reproductive parts (algae, fungi, mosses and liverworts and ferns).

The increased knowledge on anatomy, morphology and life cycles, lead to the realization that there were more natural affinities between plants, than the sexual system of Linnaeus indicated. Adanson (1763), Jussieu (1789), and Candolle (1819) all proposed various alternative natural systems that were widely followed. The ideas of natural selection as a mechanism for evolution required adaptations to the Candollean system, which started the studies on evolutionary relationships and phylogenetic classifications of plants.

A considerable amount of new knowledge today is being generated from studying model plants like *Arabidopsis thaliana*. This weedy species in the mustard family was one of the first plants to have its genome sequenced. The sequencing of the rice (*Oryza sativa*) genome and a large international research community have made rice the de facto cereal/grass/monocot model. Another grass species, *Brachypodium distachyon* is also emerging as an experimental model for understanding the genetic, cellular and molecular biology of temperate grasses. Other commercially-important staple foods like wheat, maize, barley, rye, pearl millet and soybean are also having their genomes sequenced. Some of these are challenging to sequence because they have more than two haploid (n) sets of chromosomes, a condition known as polyploidy, common in the plant kingdom. *Chlamydomonas reinhardtii* (a single-celled, green alga) is another plant model organism that has been extensively studied and provided important insights into cell biology.

In 1998 the Angiosperm Phylogeny Group published a phylogeny of flowering plants based on an analysis of DNA sequences from most families of flowering plants. As a result of this work, major questions such as which families represent the earliest branches in the genealogy of angiosperms are now understood. Investigating how plant species are related to each other allows botanists to better understand the process of evolution in plants.

Subdisciplines of Botany

- *Agronomy*—Application of plant science to crop production.
- *Bryology*—Mosses, liverworts, and hornworts.
- *Economic Botany*—The place of plants in economy.

History of Plant Systematics

The history of plant systematics—the biological classification of plants—stretches from the work of ancient Greek to modern evolutionary biologists. As a field of science, plant systematics came into being only slowly, early plant lore usually being treated as part of the study of medicine. Later, classification and description was driven by natural history and natural theology. Until the advent of the theory of evolution, nearly all classification was based on the scala naturae. The professionalization of botany in the 18th and 19th century marked a shift toward more holistic classification methods, eventually based on evolutionary relationships.

Notable Botanists

- Ibn al-Baitar (d. 1248), Andalusian-Arab scientist, botanist, pharmacist, physician, and author of one of the largest botanical encyclopedias.
- Al-Dinawari (828-896), Kurdish botanist, historian, geographer, astronomer, mathematician, and founder of Arabic botany.
- Luther Burbank (1849-1926), American botanist, horticulturist, and a pioneer in agricultural science.
- Joseph Dalton Hooker (1817-1911), English botanist and explorer. Second winner of Darwin Medal.
- Thomas Henry Huxley (1825-1895), English biologist, known as "Darwin's Bulldog" for his advocacy of Charles Darwin's theory of evolution. Third winner of Darwin Medal.
- Carl Linnaeus (1707-1778), Swedish botanist, physician and zoologist who laid the foundations for the modern scheme

of Binomial nomenclature. He is known as the father of modern taxonomy, and is also considered one of the fathers of modern ecology.

- Gregor Johann Mendel (1822-1884), Augustinian priest and scientist, and is often called the father of genetics for his study of the inheritance of traits in pea plants.
- Abu al-Abbas al-Nabati (c. 1200), Andalusian-Arab botanist and agricultural scientist, and a pioneer in experimental botany.
- Leonardo da Vinci (1452-1519), Italian polymath; a scientist, mathematician, engineer, inventor, anatomist, painter, sculptor, architect, botanist, musician and writer.
- Agustín Stahl (1842-1947), conducted investigations and experiments in the fields of ethnology, and zoology in the Caribbean region.

Early Botanical Works

Historians of botany generally begin the history of botanical classification with folk taxonomy or with Theophrastus's *Historia Plantarum*, the earliest surviving treatise on plants. Theophrastus, a student of Aristotle, did not articulate a formal classification scheme; instead he relied on the common groupings of folklore combined with growth form: tree shrub; undershrub; or herb. The *Materia medica* of Dioscorides was also an important early compendium of plant descriptions (over five hundred); it was in use from its publication in the 1st century until the 16th century. Early-modern plant classification.

In the 16th century, works by Otto Brunfels, Hieronymus Bock, and Leonhart Fuchs helped to revive interest in natural history based on first-hand observation; Bock in particular included environmental and life cycle information in his descriptions. With the influx of exotic species in the Age of Exploration, the number of known species expanded rapidly, but most authors were far more interested in the medinical properties of individual plants than an overarching classification system. Later influential Renaissance books include those of

Caspar Bauhin and Andrea Cesalpino. Bauhin described over 6000 plants, which he arranged into 12 books and 72 sections based on a wide range of common characteristics. Cesalpino based his system on the structure of the organs of fructification, using the Aristotelian technique of logical division.

In the late 17th century, the most influential classification schemes were those of English botanist and natural theologian John Ray and French botanist Joseph Pitton de Tournefort. Ray, who listed over 18,000 plant species in his works, is credited with establishing the monocot/dicot division and some of his groups—mustards, mints, legumes and grasses—stand today (though under modern family names). Tournefort used an artificial system based on logical division which was widely adopted in France and elsewhere in Europe up until Linnaeus.

The book that had an enormous accelerating effect on the science of plant systematics was the *Species Plantarum* by Linnaeus, although this work does not deal with the relationships of plants, as such. It assumed that plant species were given by God and that what remained for humans was to recognise them and use them (a Christian reformulation of the *scala naturae* or *Great Chain of Being*). The *Species Plantarum* presented a complete list of the plant species then known, ordered for the purpose of easy identification, by the number and arrangement of the male and female sexual organs of the plants. Of the groups in this book, the highest rank that continues to be used today is the genus. However, the consistent use of binomial nomenclature and the fact of having a complete listing of all plants provided a huge stimulus for the field.

Linnaeus was quite aware that the arrangement of species in the *Species Plantarum* was not a 'natural system', i.e. did not express relationships. Elsewhere Linnaeus did present some ideas of plant relationships. The earliest system of plant classification probably was that by de Jussieu (inspired on the work of Adanson) and the early nineteenth century saw the start of the work by de Candolle, culminating in the *Prodromus*.

Edible Flowers

Edible flowers are flowers that can be eaten. Just as the leaves and roots of some flowering plants can be eaten; various flowers, which can be used to decorate a room, can also be used in foods and are considered edible, often used as decoration. In addition to immediate consumption, flowers may also be preserved for future use using techniques such as drying, freezing or steeping them in oil. Edible flowers can be used in drinks, jellies, salads, soups, syrups and main dishes.

Common Edible Flowers

- Daisies (*Bellis perennis* quills)
- Dandelions (*Taraxacum officinale* leaves, roots, flowers, petals, buds)
- Daylilies (*Hemerocallis* buds, flowers, petals)
- Pansies (*Viola x Wittrockiana* flowers, petals)
- Pot Marigolds (*Calendula officinalis* petals with white heel removed)
- Nasturtium (blossoms and seeds)
- Osmanthus fragrans (flower)
- Chrysanthemum (flower)
- Roses (*Rosa* petals with white heel removed, rose hips)
- Sunflowers (*Helianthus annuus* buds, petals, seeds)
- *Sesbania grandiflora* (flower)
- Citrus blossoms (*lemon, orange, lime, grapefruit)*
- Clover
- Hibiscus
- Honeysuckle
- Jasmine (*for tea*)
- Lilac (*salads*)
- Violet ('salads')

Flower Consumption

Some general rules to follow before consuming flowers:

- If you are unsure if you have picked the correct variety of flower for the recipe, do not eat it. Some flowers are toxic and some flowers only become edible after appropriate preparations. There are many sources available to help you identify and properly prepare flowers for consumption.
- As you would with other foods, if you have food or pollen allergies, check with your doctor before consuming flowers to avoid allergic reactions.
- Always use flowers that have not been sprayed with pesticides. To accomplish this, you can either grow your own flowers or if you are purchasing flowers from a commercial grower, ask if pesticides were used in treating the flowers. Make sure the grower knows that you plan to consume the flowers.
- Do not use damaged or excessively dirty flowers. Check flowers for an overabundance of insects as this may be a sign of unsuitable flowers to consume. Wash flowers thoroughly (but gently) in cool water and dry them on paper towels.
- Always remember to remove the reproductive organs (pollen area) of the flowers if possible.
- Just because flowers are edible does not mean you should eat them at every meal. Marigolds and Daylilies for example, should be sensibly consumed.
- Do not serve edible flowers along with inedible flowers. Some guests may not know the difference and inadvertently eat an inedible flower.

As a Flavoring

The pretty blue "starflowers" of Borage can be used as a garnish and have a sweet honey-like taste.

Enjoyment of edible flowers does not have to be seasonal. Flower butter made with flower petals can be frozen for up to three months. Flower oils will also keep for up to three months.

These oils can be made with edible flower petals steeped in sunflower oil, olive oil, or other oils for about a week and then removed. Different edible flowers and oils can be used to create unique flavors. Edible flower petals can also be steeped in vinegar for three to four weeks and then removed. The flower vinegar can then be used in dressing or whenever vinegar would normally be used. Edible flowers can also be frozen with water in a standard ice-cube tray. The flower ice-cubes can be left frozen and used in drinks or any other dish that would normally contain ice-cubes. Edible flowers can be blended into sugar for about one week (and then sifted out), leaving the storable sugar flavoured for future use. Edible flowers can also be crystallized using egg white and sugar (sugar being a perservative). The candied flowers can be eaten individually or used as a garnish for a cake; and retain their colour for months.

12

Plant Physiology

INTRODUCTION

Plant physiology is a subdiscipline of botany concerned with the function, or physiology, of plants. Closely related fields include plant morphology (structure of plants), plant ecology (interactions with the environment), phytochemistry (biochemistry of plants), cell biology, and molecular biology.

Fundamental processes such as photosynthesis, respiration, plant nutrition, plant hormone functions, tropisms, nastic movements, photoperiodism, photomorphogenesis, circadian rhythms, environmental stress physiology, seed germination, dormancy and stomata function and transpiration, both part of plant water relations, are studied by plant physiologists.

The field of plant physiology includes the study of all the internal activities of plants—those chemical and physical processes associated with life as they occur in plants. This includes study at many levels of scale of size and time. At the smallest scale are molecular interactions of photosynthesis and internal diffusion of water, minerals, and nutrients. At the largest scale are the processes of plant development, seasonality, dormancy, and reproductive control. Major subdisciplines of plant physiology include phytochemistry (the study of the biochemistry of plants) and phytopathology (the study of disease in plants). The scope of plant physiology as a discipline may be divided into several major areas of research. Five key areas of study within plant physiology.

First, the study of phytochemistry (plant chemistry) is included within the domain of plant physiology. In order to function and survive, plants produce a wide array of chemical compounds not found in other organisms. Photosynthesis requires a large array of pigments, enzymes, and other compounds to function. Because they cannot move, plants must also defend themselves chemically from herbivores, pathogens and competition from other plants. They do this by producing toxins and foul-tasting or smelling chemicals. Other compounds defend plants against disease, permit survival during drought, and prepare plants for dormancy. While other compounds are used to attract pollinators or herbivores to spread ripe seeds.

Secondly, plant physiology includes the study of biological and chemical processes of individual plant cells. Plant cells have a number of features that distinguish them from cells of animals, and which lead to major differences in the way that plant life behaves and responds differently from animal life. For example, plant cells have a cell wall which restricts the shape of plant cells and thereby limits the flexibility and mobility of plants. Plant cells also contain chlorophyll, a chemical compound that interacts with light in a way that enables plants to manufacture their own nutrients rather than consuming other living things as animals do.

Thirdly, plant physiology deals with interactions between cells, tissues, and organs within a plant. Different cells and tissues are physically and chemically specialized to perform different functions. Roots and rhizoids function to anchor the plant and acquire minerals in the soil. Leaves function to catch light in order to manufacture nutrients. For both of these organs to remain living, the minerals acquired by the roots must be transported to the leaves and the nutrients manufactured in the leaves must be transported to the roots. Plants have developed a number of means by which this transport may occur, such as vascular tissue, and the functioning of the various modes of transport is studied by plant physiologists.

Fourthly, plant physiologists study the ways that plants control or regulate internal functions. Like animals, plants produce chemicals called hormones which are produced in one part of the plant to signal cells in another part of the plant to respond. Many flowering plants bloom at the appropriate time because of light-sensitive compounds that respond to the length of the night, a phenomenon known as photoperiodism. The ripening of fruit and loss of leaves in the winter are controlled in part by the production of the gas ethylene by the plant.

Finally, plant physiology includes the study of how plants respond to conditions and variation in the environment, a field known as environmental physiology. Stress from water loss, changes in air chemistry, or crowding by other plants can lead to changes in the way a plant functions. These changes may be affected by genetic, chemical, and physical factors.

Biochemistry of Plants

List of simple elements of which plants are primarily constructed—carbon, oxygen, hydrogen, calcium, phosphorus, etc.—is not different from similar lists for animals, fungi, or even bacteria. The fundamental atomic components of plants are the same as for all life; only the details of the way in which they are assembled differs.

Despite this underlying similarity, plants produce a vast array of chemical compounds with unusual properties which they use to cope with their environment. Pigments are used by plants to absorb or detect light, and are extracted by humans for use in dyes. Other plant products may be used for the manufacture of commercially important rubber or biofuel. Perhaps the most celebrated compounds from plants are those with pharmacological activity, such as salicylic acid (aspirin), morphine, and digitalis. Drug companies spend billions of dollars each year researching plant compounds for potential medicinal benefits.

Constituent Elements

Plants require some nutrients, such as carbon and nitrogen, in large quantities to survive. Such nutrients are termed macronutrients, where the prefix *macro-* (large) refers to the quantity needed, not the size of the nutrient particles themselves. Other nutrients, called micronutrients, are required only in trace amounts for plants to remain healthy. Such micronutrients are usually absorbed as ions dissolved in water taken from the soil, though carnivorous plants acquire some of their micronutrients from captured prey.

Pigments

Among the most important molecules for plant function are the pigments. Plant pigments include a variety of different kinds of molecules, including porphyrins, carotenoids, and anthocyanins. All biological pigments selectively absorb certain wavelengths of light while reflecting others. The light that is absorbed may be used by the plant to power chemical reactions, while the reflected wavelengths of light determine the color the pigment will appear to the eye.

Chlorophyll is the primary pigment in plants; it is a porphyrin that absorbs red and blue wavelengths of light while reflecting green. It is the presence and relative abundance of chlorophyll that gives plants their green colour. All land plants and green algae possess two forms of this pigment: chlorophyll *a* and chlorophyll *b*. Kelps, diatoms, and other photosynthetic heterokonts contain chlorophyll *c* instead of *b*, while red algae possess only chlorophyll *a*. All chlorophylls serve as the primary means plants use to intercept light in order to fuel photosynthesis.

Carotenoids are red, orange, or yellow tetraterpenoids. They function as accessory pigments in plants, helping to fuel photosynthesis by gathering wavelengths of light not readily absorbed by chlorophyll. The most familiar carotenoids are carotene (an orange pigment found in carrots), lutein (a yellow pigment found in fruits and vegetables), and lycopene (the red pigment responsible for the color of tomatoes). Carotenoids have been shown to act as antioxidants and to promote healthy eyesight in humans.

Anthocyanins (literally "flower blue") are water-soluble flavonoid pigments that appear red to blue, according to pH.

They occur in all tissues of higher plants, providing color in leaves, stems, roots, flowers, and fruits, though not always in sufficient quantities to be noticeable. Anthocyanins are most visible in the petals of flowers, where they may make up as much as 30% of the dry weight of the tissue. They are also responsible for the purple colour seen on the underside of tropical shade plants such as *Tradescantia zebrina*; in these plants, the anthocyanin catches light that has passed through the leaf and reflects it back towards regions bearing chlorophyll, in order to maximize the use of available light.

Betalains are red or yellow pigments. Like anthocyanins they are water-soluble, but unlike anthocyanins they are indole-derived compounds synthesized from tyrosine. This class of pigments is found only in the Caryophyllales (including cactus and amaranth), and never co-occur in plants with anthocyanins. Betalains are responsible for the deep red color of beets, and are used commercially as food-coloring agents. Plant physiologists are uncertain of the function that betalains have in plants which possess them, but there is some preliminary evidence that they may have fungicidal propertie.

Signals and Regulators

Plants produce hormones and other growth regulators which act to signal a physiological response in their tissues. They also produce compounds such as phytochrome that are sensitive to light and which serve to trigger growth or development in response to environmental signals.

Plant Hormones

Plant hormones, also known as plant growth regulators (PGRs) or phytohormones, are chemicals that regulate a plant's growth. According to a standard animal definition, hormones are signal molecules produced at specific locations, that occur in very low concentrations, and cause altered processes in target cells at other locations. Unlike animals, plants lack specific hormone-producing tissues or organs. Plant hormones are often not transported to other parts of the plant and production is not limited to specific locations.

Plant hormones are chemicals that in small amounts promote and influence the growth, development and differentiation of cells and tissues. Hormones are vital to plant growth; effecting processes in plants from flowering to seed development, dormancy, and germination. They regulate which tissues grow upwards and which grow downwards, leaf formation and stem growth, fruit development and ripening, as well as leaf abscission and even plant death.

The most important plant hormones are abscissic acid (ABA), auxins, gibberellins, and cytokinins, though there are many other substances that serve to regulate plant physiology.

Photomorphogenesis

While most people know that light is important for photosynthesis in plants, few realize that plant sensitivity to light plays a role in the control of plant structural development (morphogenesis). The use of light to control structural development is called photomorphogenesis, and is dependent upon the presence of specialized photoreceptors, which are chemical pigments capable of absorbing specific wavelengths of light.

Plants use four kinds of photoreceptors: phytochrome, cryptochrome, a UV-B photoreceptor, and protochlorophyllide *a*. The first two of these, phytochrome and cryptochrome, are photoreceptor proteins, complex molecular structures formed by joining a protein with a light-sensitive pigment. Cryptochrome is also known as the UV-A photoreceptor, because it absorbs ultraviolet light in the long wave "A" region. The UV-B receptor is one or more compounds that have yet to be identified with certainty, though some evidence suggests carotene or riboflavin as candidates. Protochlorophyllide *a*, as its name suggests, is a chemical precursor of chlorophyll.

The most studied of the photoreceptors in plants is phytochrome. It is sensitive to light in the red and far-red region of the visible spectrum. Many flowering plants use it to regulate the time of flowering based on the length of day and night (photoperiodism) and to set circadian rhythms. It also regulates other responses including the germination of seeds, elongation of seedlings, the size, shape and number of leaves, the synthesis of chlorophyll, and the straightening of the epicotyl or hypocotyl hook of dicot seedlings.

Photoperiodism

Many flowering plants use the pigment phytochrome to sense seasonal changes in day length, which they take as signals to flower. This sensitivity to day length is termed photoperiodism. Broadly speaking, flowering plants can be classified as long day plants, short day plants, or day neutral plants, depending on thir particular response to changes in day length. Long day plants require a certain minimum length of daylight to initiate flowering, so these plants flower in the spring or summer. Conversely, short day plants will flower when the length of daylight falls below a certain critical level. Day neutral plants do not initiate flowering based on photoperiodism, though some may use temperature sensitivity (vernalization) instead.

Although a short day plant cannot flower during the long days of summer, it is not actually the period of light exposure that limits flowering. Rather, a short day plant requires a minimal length of uninterrupted darkness in each 24 hour period (a short daylength) before floral development can begin. It has been determined experimentally that a short day plant (long night) will not flower if a flash of phytochrome activiting light is used on the plant during the night.

Plants make use of the phytochrome system to sense day length or photoperiod. This fact is utilized by florists and greenhouse gardeners to control and even induce flowering out of season, such as the *Poinsettia*.

Environmental Physiology

Paradoxically, the subdiscipline of environmental physiology is on the one hand a recent field of study in plant ecology and on the other hand one of the oldest. Environmental phyiology is the preferred name of the subdiscipline among plant physiologists, but it goes by a number of other names in the applied sciences. It is roughly synonymous with ecophysiology, crop ecology, horticulture, and agronomy. The particular name applied to the subdiscipline is specific to the viewpoint and goals of research. Whatever name is applied, it deals with the ways in which plants respond to their environment and so overlaps with the field of ecology.

Environmental physiologists examine plant response to physical factors such as radiation (including light and ultraviolet radiation), temperature, fire, and wind. Of particular importance are water relations and the stress of drought or inundation, exchange of gases with the atmosphere, as well as the cycling of nutrients such as nitrogen and carbon. Environmental physiologists also examine plant response to biological factors. This includes not only negative interactions, such as competition, herbivory, disease, and parasitism, but also positive interactions, such as mutualism and pollination.

Tropisms and Nastic Movements

Plants may respond both to directional and nondirectional stimuli. A response to a directional stimulus, such as gravity or sunlight, is called a tropism. A response to a nondirectional stimulus, such as temperature or humidity, is a nastic movement.

Tropisms in plants are the result of differential cell growth, in which the cells on one side of the plant elongate more than those on the other side, causing the part to bend toward the side with less growth. Among the common tropisms seen in plants is phototropism, the bending of the plant toward a source of light. Phototropism allows the plant to maximize light exposure in plants which require additional light for photosynthesis, or to minimize it in plants subjected to intense light and heat. Geotropism allows the roots of a plant to determine the direction of gity and grow downwards. Tropisms generally result from an interaction between the environment and production of one or more plant hormones. In contrast to tropisms, nastic movements result from changes in turgor pressure within plant tissues, and may occur rapidly. A familiar example is thigmonasty (response to touch) in the Venus fly trap, a carnivorous plant. The traps consist of modified leaf blades which bear sensitive trigger hairs. When the hairs are touched by an insect or other animal, the leaf folds shut. This mechanism allows the plant to trap and digest small insects for additional nutrients. Although the trap is rapidly shut by changes in internal cell pressures, the leaf must grow slowly in order to reset for a second opportunity to trap insects.

Plant Disease

Economically, one of the most important areas of research in environmental physiology is that of phytopathology, the study of diseases in plants and the manner in which plants resist or cope with infection. Plant are susceptible to the same kinds of disease organisms as animals, including viruses, bacteria, and fungi, as well as physical invasion by insects and roundworms.

Because the biology of plants differs from animals, their symptoms and responses are quite different. In some cases, a plant can simply shed infected leaves or flowers to prevent to spread of disease, in a process called abscission. Most animals do not have this option as a means of controlling disease. Plant diseases organisms themselves also differ from those causing disease in animals because plants cannot usually spread infection through casual physical contact. Plant pathogens tend to spread via spores or are carried by animal vectors.

One of the most important advances in the control of plant disease was the discovery of Bordeaux mixture in the nineteenth century. The mixture is the first known fungicide and is a combination of copper sulfate and lime. Application of the mixture served to inhibit the growth of downy mildew that threatened to seriously damage the French wine industry.

Sir Francis Bacon published one of the first plant physiology experiments in 1627 in the book, *Sylva Sylvarum.* Bacon grew several terrestrial plants, including a rose, in water and concluded that soil was only needed to keep the plant upright. Jan Baptist van Helmont published what is considered the first quantitative experiment in plant physiology in 1648. He grew a willow tree for five years in a pot containing 200 pounds of oven-dry soil. The soil lost just two ounces of dry weight and van Helmont concluded that plants get all their weight from water, not soil. In 1699, John Woodward published experiments on growth of spearmint in different sources of water. He found that plants grew much better in water with soil added than in distilled water.

Stephen Hales is considered the Father of Plant Physiology for the many experiments in the 1727 book; though Julius von Sachs unified the pieces of plant physiology and put them together as a discipline. His *Lehrbuch der Botanik* was the plant physiology bible of its time.

Researchers discovered in the 1800s that plants absorb essential mineral nutrients as inorganic ions in water. In natural conditions, soil acts as a mineral nutrient reservoir but the soil itself is not essential to plant growth. When the mineral nutrients in the soil are dissolved in water, plant roots absorb nutrients readily, soil is no longer required for the plant to thrive. This observation is the basis for hydroponics, the growing of plants in a water solution rather than soil, which has become a standard technique in biological research, teaching lab exercises, crop production and as a hobby.

Current Research

One of the leading journals in the field is *Plant Physiology*, started in 1926. All its back issues are available online for free. Many other journals often carry plant physiology articles, including *Physiologia Plantarum, Journal of Experimental Botany, American Journal of Botany, Annals of Botany, Journal of Plant Nutrition* and *Proceedings of the National Academy of Sciences.*

Economic Applications

In horticulture and agriculture along with food science, plant physiology is an important topic relating to fruits, vegetables, and other consumable parts of plants. Topics studied include: *climatic* requirements, fruit drop, nutrition, ripening, fruit set. The production of food crops also hinges on the study of plant physiology covering such topics as optimal planting and harvesting times and post harvest storage of plant products for human consumption and the production of secondary products like drugs and cosmetics.

13

Plant Sexuality

INTRODUCTION

Among all living organisms, flowers which are the reproductive structures of angiosperms, are the most varied physically and show the greatest diversity in methods of reproduction of all biological systems Carolus Linnaeus proposed a system of classification of flowering plants based on plant structures, since plants employ many different morphological adaptations involving sexual reproduction, flowers played an important role in that classification system. Later on Christian Konrad Sprengel studied plant sexuality and called it the "revealed secret of nature" and for the first time it was understood that the pollination process involved both biotic and abiotic interactions (Charles Darwin's theories of natural selection utilized this work to promote his idea of evolution). Plants that are not flowering plants (green alga, mosses, liverworts, hornworts, ferns, and gymnosperms) also have complex interplays between morphological adaptation and environmental factors in their sexual reproduction. The breeding system, or how the sperm from one plant fertilizes the ovals of another, is the single most important determinant of the mating structure of nonclonal plant populations. The mating structure or morphology of the flower parts and their arrangement on the plant in turn controls the amount and distribution of genetic variation, a central element in the evolutionary process.

History

Unlike animals, plants are immobile and cannot seek out sexual partners for reproduction. The first plants used abiotic means to transport sperm for reproduction, utilizing water and wind. The first plants were aquatic and released sperm freely into the water to be carried by the currents. As plants moved onto land they used a thin film of water or water droplets like liverworts and ferns, in which mobile sperm swam from the male reproduction organs to the female organs. As plants became more complex and developed vascular systems enabling them to grow taller, they used alternation of generations like in ferns or the wind to move spores. In the Paleozoic era progymnosperms reproduced by using spores dispersed on the wind, 350 million years ago the seed plants evolved, including seed ferns, conifers and cordaites all were gymnosperms. Pollen grains, the male gametophyte, developed for protection of the sperm during the process of transfer from male to female parts. It is believed that insects feed on the pollen and plants evolved to use insects to actively carry pollen from one plant to the next. Seed producing plants, which include the angiosperms and the gymnosperms, have hetromorphic alternation of generations with large sporophytes containing much reduced gametophytes. Angiosperms have distinctive reproductive organs called flowers with carpels and the gametophyte is greatly reduced to a female embryo sac with as few as eight cells and the male gametophyte develop from the pollen grains. The sperm of seed plants are non motile except for two older groups of plants the Cycadophyta and the Ginkgophyta which have flagellated sperm.

Terminology

The flowers of angiosperms are determinate shoots that have sporophylls. The parts of flowers are named by scientists and show great variation in shape, these flower parts include sepals, petals, stamens and carpels. As a group the sepals form the calyx and as a group the petals form the corolla, together the corolla and the calyx is called the perianth. The stamens collectively are called the androecuim and the carpels collectively are called the gynoecium.

The complexity of the systems and devices used by plants to achieve sexual reproduction has resulted in botanists and evolutionary biologists using numerous terms to describe physical structures and functional strategies. Dellaporta and Calderon-Urrea (1993) list and define a variety of terms used to describe the modes of sexuality at different levels in flowering plants. This list is reproduced here generalized to fit more than just plants that have flowers, and expanded to include other terms and more complete definitions.

Individual Reproductive Unit (A Flower in Angiosperms)

Bisexual - or perfect flowers have both male (androecium) and female (gynoecium) reproductive parts, including stamens, carpels, and an ovary. Flowers that contain both androecium and gynoecium are called androgynous or hermaphroditic. Examples of plants with perfect or bisexual flowers include the lily, rose, and most plants with large showy flowers, though a perfect flower does not have to have petals or sepals. Other terms widely used are:

- hermaphrodite;
- monoclinous; and
- synoecious.

Unisexual - Reproductive structure that is either functionally male or functionally female. In angiosperms this condition is also called diclinous, imperfect or incomplete.

Adaptations

Typically large amounts of pollen are produced and pollination often occurs early in the growing season before leaves can interfere with the dispersal of the pollen. Many trees and all grasses and sedges are wind pollinated, as such they have no need for large fancy flowers. In plants that use insects or other animals to move pollen from one flower to the next, plants have developed greatly modified flower parts to attract pollinators and to facilitate the movement of pollen from one flower to the insect and from the insect back to the next flower. Plants have a number of different means to attract pollinators including color, scent, heat, nectar glands, eatable pollen and flower shape. Along with modifications involving the above structures two other conditions play a very important role in the sexual reproduction of flowering plants, the first is timing of flowering and the other is the size or number of flowers produced. Often plant species have a few large, very showy flower while others produce many small flower, often flowers are collected together into large inflorescences to maximize their visual effect, becoming more noticeable to passing by pollinators. Flowers are attraction strategies and sexual expressions are functional strategies used to produce the next generation of plants, with pollinators and plants having co-evolved, often to some extraordinary degrees, very often mutually benefiting both.

The largest family of flowering plants is the orchids (Orchidaceae), estimated by some specialists to include up to 35,000 species, which often have highly specialized flowers used to attract insects and facilitate pollination. The stamens are modified to produce pollen in clusters called pollinium, which are attached to insects when crawling into the flower. The flower shapes are modified to force insects to pass by the pollen, which is "glued" to the insect. Some orchids are even more highly specialized, with flower shapes that mimic the shape of insects to attract them to 'mate' with the flowers, a few even have scents that mimic insect pheromones.

Another large group of flowering plants is the Asteraceae or sunflower family with close to 22,000 species, which also have highly modified inflorescences that are flowers collected together in heads composed of a composite of individual flowers called florets. Heads with florets of one sex, when the flowers are pistillate or functionally staminate, or made up of all bisexual florets, are called homogamous and can include discoid and liguliflorous type heads. Some radiate heads may be homogamous too. Plants with heads that have florets of two or more sexual forms are called heterogamous and include radiate and disciform head forms, though some radiate heads may be heterogamous too.

Individual Plant Sexuality

Many plants have complete flowers that have both male and female parts, others only have male or female parts and still other plants have flowers on the same plant that are a mix of male and female flowers. Some plants even have mixes that include all three types of flowers, where some flowers are only male, some are only female and some are both male and female. A distinction needs to be made between arrangements of sexual parts and the expression of sexuality in single plants verses the species. Some plants also undergo what is called Sex-switching, like *Arisaema triphyllum* which express sexual differences at different stages of growth. In some arums smaller plants produce all or mostly male flowers and as plants grow larger over the years the male flowers are replaced by more female flowers on the same plant. *Arisaema triphyllum* thus covers a multitude of sexual conditions in its life time; from nonsexual juvenile plants to young plants that are all male, as plants grow larger they have a mix of both male and female flowers, to large plants that have mostly female flowers. Other species have plants that produce more male flowers early in the year and as plants bloom later in the growing season they produce more female flowers. In plants like *Thalictrum dioicum* all the plants in the species are ether male or female.

Specific terms:

- ***Androecious:*** plants producing male flowers only, produce pollen but no seeds, the male plants of a Dioecious species.
- ***Dioecious:*** having unisexual reproductive units with male and female plants.(flowers, conifer cones, or functionally equivalent structures) occurring on different individuals; from Greek for "two households". Individual plants are not called dioecious: they are either gynoecious (female plants) or androecious (male plants).
- ***Gynoecious:*** plants producing female flowers only, produces seeds but no pollen, the female of a Dioecious species. In some plant species or populations all individuals are gynoecious with non sexual reproduction used to produce the next generation.

- *Hermaphrodite:* A plant that has only bisexual reproductive units (flowers, conifer cones, or functionally equivalent structures). In angiosperm terminology a synonym is **monoclinous** from the Greek "one bed".
- *Monoecious:* having separate male and female reproductive units (flowers, conifer cones, or functionally equivalent structures) on the same plant; from Greek for "one household". Individuals bearing separate flowers of both sexes at the same time are called simultaneously or synchronously monoecious. Individuals that bear flowers of one sex at one time are called consecutively monoecious; Plants may first have single sexed flowers and then later have flowers of the other sex. *Protoandrous* describes individuals that function first as males and then change to females; *protogynous* describes individuals that function first as females and then change to males.
- *Subdioecious,* a tendency in some dioecious species to produce monoecious plants. The population produces normally male or female plants but some are hermaphroditic, with female plants producing some male or hermaphroditic flowers or vise versa. The condition is thought to represent a transition between hermaphroditism and dioecy.
- *Gynomonoecious:* has both hermaphrodite and female structures.
- *Andromonoecious:* has both hermaphrodite and male structures.
- *Subandroecious*: plant has mostly male flowers, with a few female or hermaphrodite flowers.
- *Subgynoecious:* plant has mostly female flowers, with a few male or hermaphrodite flowers.
- *Trimonoecious* (polygamous): male, female, and hermaphrodite structures all appear on the same plant.
- *Diclinous* ("two beds"), an angiosperm term, includes all species with unisexual flowers, although particularly those with *only* unisexual flowers, i.e. the monoecious and dioecious species.

Holly (*Ilex aquifolium*) is dioecious: (above) shoot with flowers from male plant; (top right) male flower enlarged, showing stamens with pollen and reduced, sterile stigma; (below) shoot with flowers from female plant; (lower right) female flower enlarged, showingstigma and reduced, sterile stamens with no pollen.

Plant Population

Most often plants show uniform strategies across the species or in populations in their sexual expression and specific terms are used to describe the sexual expression of the species or population.

- *Hermaphrodite:* only hermaphrodite plants with flowers that have both male and female parts.
- *Monoecious:* only monoecious plants, that is plants have separate male and female flowers on the same plant. A plant species where the male and female organs are found in different flowers on the same plant, often plants are wind pollinated like some trees and grasses like corn.
- *Dioecious:* only dioecious plants, all plants are either female or male.
- *Gynodioecious:* both female and hermaphrodite plants present. In some plants, strictly female plants are produced by the degeneration of the tapetum, a shell-like structure in the anther of a flower where the pollen cells form, producing male sterility.
- *Gynoecy:* plants are all females in a population, often regulated by environmental factors like temperature, photo period or water availability.
- *Androdioecious:* both male and hermaphrodite plants present.
- *Polygamous:* when there is a mix of hermaphrodite and unisexual plants in the natural population.
- *Subdioecious:* population of unisexual (dioecious) plants, with monoecious individuals too.

- *Trioecious:* sometimes used in place of subdioecious when male, female, and hermaphrodite plants are more equally mixed with in the same population.

About 11% of all angiosperms are strictly dioecious or monoecious, Intermediate forms of sexual dimorphism, including gynodioecy and androdioecy, represent 7% of the species examined of a survey of 120,000 plant species. In the same survey, 10% of the species contain both unisexual and bisexual flowers.

The majority of plant species use allogamy - also called cross-pollination, as a means of breeding. Many plants are self fertile and the male parts can pollinate the female parts of the same flower and/or same plant. Some plants use a method known as self-incompatibility to promote outcrossing. In these plants, the male organs cannot fertilize the female parts of the same plant, other plants produce male and female flowers at different times to promote outcrossing. Some plants have bisexual flowers but the pollen is produced before the stigma of the same flower is receptive of pollen, this promotes out crossing by greatly limiting self pollination and these types of flowers are called *protandrous.*

Flower Morphology

A species such as the ash tree (*Fraxinus excelsior* L.), demonstrates the possible range of variation in morphology and functionality exhibited by flowers with respect to gender. Flowers of the ash are wind-pollinated and lack petals and sepals. Structurally, the flowers may be either male or female, or even hermaphroditic, consisting of two anthers and an ovary. A male flower can be morphologically male or hermaphroditic, with anthers and a rudimentary gynoecium. Ash flowers can also be morphologically female, or hermaphroditic and functionally female.

Evolution

Angiosperms

It is thought that flowering plants evolved from a common hermaphrodite ancestor, and that dioecy evolved from hermaphroditism. Hermaphroditism is very common in flowering plants; over 85% are hermaphroditic, whereas only about 6-7% are dioecious and 5-6% are monoecious.

A fair degree of correlation (though far from complete) exists between dioecy/sub-dioecy and plants that have seeds dispersed by birds (both nuts and berries). It is hypothesized that the concentration of fruit in half of the plants increases dispersal efficiency; female plants can produce a higher density of fruit as they do not expend resources on pollen production, and the dispersal agents (birds) need not waste time looking for fruit on male plants. Other correlations with dioecy include: tropical distribution, woody growth form, perenniality, fleshy fruits, and small, green flowers.

Plant growth regulators can be used to alter flower and plant sexuality, in cucumbers ethephon is used to delay staminate flowering and transforms monoecious lines into all-pistillate or female lines. Gibberellins also increase maleness in cucumbers. Cytokinins have been used in grapes that have undeveloped pistils to produce functional female organs and seed formation.

Plant Anatomy

Plant anatomy or phytotomy is the general term for the study of the internal structure of plants. While originally it included plant morphology, which is the description of the physical form and external structure of plants, since the mid Twentieth Century the investigation of plant anatomy is considered a separate, distinct field, and refers to just the internal plant structures. Plant anatomy is now frequently investigated at the cellular level, and often involves the sectioning of tissues and microscopy.

History

About 300 BCE Theophrastus wrote a number of plant treatises, only two of which survive. He developed concepts of plant morphology and classification, which did not withstand the scientific scrutiny of the Renaissance.

A Swiss physician and botanist, Gaspard Bauhin, introduced binomial nomenclature into plant taxonomy. He published *Pinax theatri botanici* in 1596, which was the first to use this convention for naming of species. His criteria for classification included natural relationships, or 'affinities', which in many cases were structural.

Italian doctor and microscopist, Marcello Malpighi, was one of the two founders of plant anatomy. In 1671 he published his *Anatomia Plantarum*, the first major advance in plant physiogamy since Aristotle.

The British doctor, Nehemiah Grew was one of the two founders of plant anatomy. He published *An Idea of a Philosophical History of Plants* in 1672 and *The Anatomy of Plants* in 1682. Grew is credited with the recognition of plant cells, although he called them 'vesicles' and 'bladders'. He correctly identified and described the sexual organs of plants (flowers) and their parts.

In the Eighteenth Century, Carolus Linnaeus established taxonomy based on structure, and his early work was with plant anatomy. While the exact structural level which is to be considered to be scientifically valid for comparison and differentiation has changed with the growth of knowledge, the basic principles were established by Linnaeus. He published his master work, *Species Plantarum* in 1753.

In 1802, French botanist, Charles-François Brisseau de Mirbel, published *Traité d'anatomie et de physiologie végétale* (*Treatise on Plant Anatomy and Physiology*) establishing the beginnings of the science of plant cytology.

In 1812, Johann Jacob Paul Moldenhawer published *Beyträge zur Anatomie der Pflanzen*, describing microscopic studies of plant tissues.

In 1813 a Swiss botanist, Augustin Pyrame de Candolle, published *Théorie élémentaire de la botanique*, in which he argued that plant anatomy, not physiology, ought to be the sole basis for plant classification. Using a scientific basis, he established structural criteria for defining and separating plant genera.

In 1830, Franz Meyen published *Phytotomie,* the first comprehensive review of plant anatomy.

In 1838 German botanist, Matthias Jakob Schleiden, published *Contributions to Phytogenesis,* stating, "the lower plants all consist of one cell, while the higher plants are composed of (many) individual cells" thus confirming and continuing Mirabel's work.

A German-Polish botanist, Eduard Strasburger, described the mitotic process in plant cells and further demonstrated that new cell nuclei can only arise from the division of other pre-existing nuclei. His *Studien über Protoplasma* was published in 1876.

Gottlieb Haberlandt, a German botanist, studied plant physiology and classified plant tissue based upon function. On this basis, in 1884 he published *Physiologische Pflanzenanatomie* (*Physiological Plant Anatomy*) in which he described twelve types of tissue systems (absorptive, mechanical, photosynthetic, etc.).

British paleobotanists Dunkinfield Henry Scott and William Crawford Williamson described the structures of fossilized plants at the end of the Nineteenth Century. Scott's *Studies in Fossil Botany* was published in 1900.

Following Charles Darwin's *Origin of Species* a Canadian botanist, Edward Charles Jeffrey, who was studying the comparative anatomy and phylogeny of different vascular plant groups, applied the theory to plants using the form and structure of plants to establish a number of evolutionary lines. He published his *The Anatomy of Woody Plants* in 1917.

The growth of comparative plant anatomy was spearheaded by a British botanist, Agnes Arber. She published *Water Plants: A Study of Aquatic Angiosperms* in 1920, *Monocotyledons: A Morphological Study* in 1925, and *The Gramineae: A Study of Cereal, Bamboo and Grass* in 1934.

14

Plant Sciences

INTRODUCTION

Botany is a mother science which has given birth to several branches, each being pursued as a speciality. The study of botany has undergone a tremendous change in the past 50 years and is presently called Plant Sciences to cover its wide scope. Early contributions to botanical knowledge were mainly made in colleges and universities by eminent individuals, who were fired by a spirit ofnationalism. By talent and devotion they built schools of botanical learning. Undoubtedly, India has worldwide recognition in embryology, palaeobotany, taxonomy, cytology, cytogenetics, plant breeding, plant tissue culture and morphogenesis, and ecology. I.H. Burkill has compiled *Chapters on History of Botany in India*. B.M. Johri has edited two volumes on *Botany in India: History and Progress*, sponsored by the INSA.

Reproductive Biology

Adiscipline in which India holds leadership in the botanical world is embryology, nurtured by P. Maheshwari at Agra, Dacca and Delhi. *An Introduction to the Embryology of Angiosperms* authored by him in 1950 was, for many years, an authoritative textbook used the world over. Several important works such as *Embryology of Angiosperms* and *Comparative Embryology of Angiosperms*, by other authors have appeared since then. Besides investigating the embryology of seed plants of diverse families, and using the data generated for comparative and evolutionary purposes, outstanding contributions have been made in experimental embryology such as test-tube fertilization, pollen-pistil interaction, sexual-incompatibility, wide hybridization, nucellus and endosperm culture. In pollen biology the Indian endeavour covers morphology, aerobiology in relation to allergies, pollen viability, storage, germination and more recently biotechnology.

In plants that bear fruits with numerous seeds, there is intense competition among seeds for resources. It is only recently that studies have been initiated towards the understanding of concepts such as clutch-size, sibling-rivalry, parent-offspring conflict and neighbourhood effect by researchers at the University of Agricultural Sciences (UAS), Bangalore, India. These authors have provided recent evidence that only one out of 30 potential seeds develop in the *Jamun* tree (*Syzygium cumini*). The dominant seed draws the nutrients at the expense of the others. It also produces a chemical inhibitor (an indole compound) that suppresses the subordinate seeds.

It is regrettable that reproductive biology, especially breeding systems and gene flow in the identification of reproductive constraints, has not been studied in India in many economically important plants, including forest trees (except at a few centres such as Chandigarh, Jammu, Lucknow, Waltair and Delhi). For any tree-breeding programme, basic information on reproductive biology is essential. For instance a study made at Delhi on reproduction by seed in the ancient Indian medicinal plant guggul (*Commiphora wightii*) showed that the plant is a nonpseudogamous apomict (not involving male participation) with nucellar polyembryony followed by autonomous endosperm development. Apomixis—the formation of seeds without fertilization—occurs in many grasses, dandelions and parthenium. Apomixis is now being studied at the molecular level with the hope that any gene(s) that regulate it might be introduced to fix hybrid vigour, to save time, labour and money. Genes which confer apomixis act at the stage of female meiosis. Therefore, it is essential to ultimately engineer apomixis in crop plants.

Scientists at the CCMB have discovered a novel gene called *DYAD* in *Arabidopsis* which is involved in the control of female meiosis in plants.

PALAEOBOTANY

Pioneering research work has been done at the Birbal Sahni Institute of Palaeobotany, Lucknow The creation of a new order Pentoxylales, a group of Jurassic fossil gymnosperms from Rajmahal hills in Bihar, India; verification of Wagner's theory of continental drift, providing scientific evidence for the Himalayan uplift, studies on stratigraphy relating to the classification of the Gondwanas; and origin, composition and reconstruction of the *Glossopteris* flora are some of the contributions which have received international ecognition. Pollen with angiospermoid characters have been described from intertrappean sediments of Rajmahal basin (118 Ma). Besides reporting fossils of wild seeded banana and coconut, the Indian palaeobotanists have proved that the present Kutch regionhad luxuriant moist evergreen to deciduous vegetation.

The earliest record of a mango fossil leaf from north-east India dates back to 55 Ma. Analysis of microfossils has enabled palaeobotanists to answer questions that have a bearing on coal, oil and natural gas. Other contributions of Indian palaeobotanists relate to changing palaeoclimates, migratory pathways of plants and causes of mass extinction. Coccoid and rod-shaped bacteria have been discovered in the sediments of Kudremukh iron formation, dating back to 2.6 billion years. The early photosynthetic, oxygen producing cyanobacteria isolated from stromatolites are also dated 2.6 billion years.

Biodiversity and Systematics

India is one of the 12 megadiversity countries and has all the 13 biomes found in the world, with two major hotspots out of a total of eighteen. Importantly, India is one of the global centres for domesticated biodiversity (accounting for 160 domesticated species including rice, beans, sugarcane, citrus, mango, banana, eggplant, black pepper and cucumber). The approximate total number of plant species (including fungi and bacteria) recorded until now is between 45,000 and 49,000. These are distributed in the following groups: Angiosperms (flowering plants) 15,000-17,000; Gymnosperms 64; Pteridophytes 1,022; Bryophytes 3,700;Lichens 2,400; Fungi 23,000; Algae 2,500 and Bacteria 1,000. The exact numbers are not yet finally established. Among these there are 5,100 endemics in angiosperms (1,600 in Western Ghats and 3,500 in Eastern Himalaya). About 2000 species are threatened. Out of 120 endangered species, 60 are prioritized for conservation.

Non-Vascular Cryptogams

Indian botanists have carved a name for themselves in world botany for their studies on algae from soils, fresh water and marine environments. Whereas the school of Algae at Madras University led by M.O.P. Iyengar made extensive collections of marine brown and red algae, some of his students took up studies on the bluegreen algae or Cyanophyceae (now termed Cyanobacteria) and diatoms and wrote authoritative monographs. At the Banaras Hindu University (BHU) Y. Bharadwaja and R.N. Singh and their students specialized in the taxonomy, ecology and cytology of algae, physiology (notably nitrogen fixation), genetics and cytology. The first reports of the occurrence of viruses in thebluegreens and genetic recombination were from BHU using antibiotic-resistant mutants of *Anacystis nidulans.* The presence of plasmids and the role of UV radiation on growth, survival, adaptation and mutagenesis were also established for the first timeat BHU. Other centres of algal research are at Allahabad, Lucknow, Jammu and Mysore. Applied aspects (such as extraction of biologically important compounds) from marine algae and use of bluegreen algae for scavenging toxic substances and heavy metals are being pursued at several centres.

More than 2000 fungal genera accounting for 1/5 of the total global representation of fungi are reported from India. An enormous amount of work has been done on the taxonomy, morphology, reproduction, physiology, pathology (T.S. Sadasivan), genetics and industrial aspects of fungi(M.J. Thirumalachar). One hundred and eighty-five new genera of fungi have been described. The largest number belong to Deuteromycotina.

Authoritative works have been published onHyphomycetes, Myxomycetes and Clavariaceae (K.S. Thind). The physiology of parasitism and mechanism of resistance to fungal diseases have been pursued at the universitites of Madras, Calcutta and Allahabad (R.N. Tandon). The role of mycorrhizae (both ectotrophic and VAM) in the improvement of plant nutrition (especially phosphorus uptake), drought tolerance, suppression of soil-borne pathogens and reclamation of derelict lands are important current activities at UAS, Bangalore; Osmania University, Hyderabad; and University of Delhi (Delhi). The study of lichens was neglected until 1947. The pioneering efforts done at Lucknow, Pune and Kolkata have shown that over 2,000 species occurin India.

Bryophytes, the first plants to migrate from water to land are evolutionarily and ecologically significant. India accounts for nearly 18% of the worldÕs bryophytes. The Lahore School of Bryophytes established by S.R. Kashyap was continued by his students, P. N. Mehra and R.S. Chopra at Chandigarh and by S.K. Pande at Lucknow. The evolutionary theories put forth by Mehra on the origin of thalloid forms from the foliose habit and evolution of the marchantiaceous thallus have been highly valued in academic circles. Cytotaxonomic work on mosses (Chandigarh) and taxonomy and palynology of the bryophytes by Ram Udar at Lucknow have resulted in landmark publications. At the Calcutta University, Gangulee took up the assiduous task of compiling the monumental work, *The Mosses of Eastern India and Adjacent Regions* (1969-80) in eight fasciles. The best known fossil liverworts (notably *Hepaticites nidpurensis*) were described from the Triassic beds of India by D.D. Pant.

Bryophytes have been used for ecological, geobotanical and geochemical studies in KumaonHimalaya. They are also excellent materials for experimental studies on morphogenesis, physiology and molecular biology. Notable among the Indiancontributions are studies on: (i) control of spore germination; (ii) auxin regulation of protonemal differentiation from chloronema to caulonema and its regulation by cyclic AMP(at TIFR) Bombay; (iii) bud induction and formation of gemmae. Severalother investigations include control of apogamy,apospory and sexuality by light, tempertaure and plant growth regulators (PGRs) and sugars includedin the medium; and (iv) production of antibiotics.

Pteridophytes and Gymnosperms

Ferns and fernallies (Pteridophytes) ruled the dynasty of plant world during the carboniferous age (325 millionyears ago) as giant lycopods. They have now been relegated to a secondary position in botanical hierarchy. Over 82 species of Indian pteridophytes are vulnerable or extinct. Besides their important role in phytosociology, they are prized for their high ornamental value. The fascinating aspect that has attracted evolutionists to pteridophytes, both living and fossil, is incipient heterospory, leading to seed habit.

Azolla, the tiny aquatic fern harbours *Anabaena azollae,* a nitrogen fixing cyanobacterium in its pouches. Its role as a biofertilizer in tropical paddy fields has been studied at Varanasi and Cuttack.

Plant scientists at Chandigarh and Patiala have carried out extensive work on the cytotaxonomy and ecology of pteridophytes. They have also started the *Indian Fern Journal.* Other active groups engaged in research which have added substantially to our knowledge of taxonomy, palynotaxonomy and reproductive biology of this group are from the National Botanical Research Institute (NBRI), Lucknow, and from universities of Lucknow, Allahabad, Panjab, Punjabi (at Patiala) and Calicut.

Pteridophytes have also served as model systems for understanding morphogenesis. Several live collections of ferns and their allies have been conserved in botanical gardens in the above mentioned institutions. Owing to habitat destruction and over-collection by botanists and horticulturists, pteridophytes such as *Psilotum* and tree ferns have become rare and endangered at several original sites. Gymnosperms are seed-bearing plants that lack fruits. They constitute a major component of the Himalayan forests as conifers. Cycads and gnetopsids are important groups in the study of plant evolution. B. Sahni's creation of a new group of fossil plants—the Pentoxylales—is a fundamental contribution to the field of gymnosperms.

Befittingly *Pentoxylon sahnii* features in the emblem of the Birbal Sahni Institute of Palaeobotany (BSIP) and of the journal *The Palaeobotanist*.

Scientists of BSIP, D.D. Pant and his students at Allahabad, and U. Sen and his collaborators at Kolkata have enriched our knowledge of *Glossopteris* flora, Mesozoic gymnosperms and palynology. Structural, embryological, cytological aspects, and cytogenetical evolution, genetic architecture and taxonomic accounts of extant gymnosperms have been studied by researchers at Delhi, Lucknow, Chandigarh (P.N. Mehra), Allahabad, Chennai (B.G.L. Swamy) and Bangalore.

Monographs and books have been prepared on *Abies, Cedrus, Picea, Pinus, Gnetum*, and *Ephedra*. Studies on population structure and reproductive biology, with special reference to breeding system in pines have been carried out by P. D. Dogra. The cycads, often called living fossils, are disappearing from their natural habitats in India and need special efforts for conservation.

Angiosperms

The Botanical Survey of India (BSI) with its headquarters in Kolkata and nine circles was, has been, and will be the nucleus for preparing an inventory of plant resources of the country. This is a stupendous task and will have to be shared by teachers and scholars in colleges and universities and professionals in other institutions. The major achievements of BSI in the post-Independence era are the launching of a 35-volume *Flora of India* project, of which six have been published.

Numerous local, district and state floras have appeared. The BSI has a chain of 11 herbaria, of largest. The total holdings in the BSI herbaria exceed 2.48 million, including 11,892 precious type specimens of the Indian Flora. Computerization of the herbarium sheets has been started by BSI. On the basis of floristic/ taxonomic studies since 1964, over 1,500 taxa new to India and about 700 plants new to science, including over 26 genera have been added. After careful evaluation of the status and threat perceptions, Red Data Sheets on 1,182 species have been compiled. Data on 708 are available in print.

It is paradoxical that when there is serious global concern for the conservation of biodiversity, India should face an acute shortage of experts who can study, evaluate and explain the role of the wide variety of organisms in nature. The teaching of taxonomy is being neglected and taxonomists are undervalued not only in society but even in cientific circles. However, a few dedicated taxonomists have been relentlessly taking up loristic surveys and taxonomic studies. They have brought to light not only new species but have also uncovered several plants reported to be either xtinct or extremely rare. Some of their contributions are: *Flora of Ladakh, Alpine Flora of Kashmir Himalaya, Flora of Indian Desert, Flora of Meghalaya, Flora of Tamil Nadu Carnatic and Excursion Flora (Tamil Nadu), The Flora of Karnataka* (two volumes), *Flora of Silent Valley, Flora of Udupi District, Flora of District Garhwal* and *Flora of Shimoga District.*

The family Hydatellaceae (so far thought to be endemic to Australia) has been reported to occur in Maharashtra. As a signatory to the Convention on Biological Diversity (CBD) held in Rio de Janerio in 1992, it was obligatory for India to commit itself to capacity building in taxonomy and take up exploration and preparation of an inventory of living organisms.

Training in plant and animal biosystematics has also been recognized as an important component. The taxonomic issues that need to be addressed in this century are mostly those that require interfacing of systematics and other disciplines.

These include bioprospecting, conservation biology, ecosystem management and bioremediation. The other priority issues to be probed are inventorying and monitoring of plant diversity, particularly in areas which are unexplored, assessment of conservation status of species and roles of species in communities and ecosystems.

Cytology

Early efforts were addressed to the enumeration of chromosome number, size and karyotype of plants belonging to various groups at Chandigarh, Kolkata, Waltair, NBRI, BHU, Dharwar, etc. Cytological information has been used as a criterion for evolution and genotoxicology. The book *Chromosome Techniques: Theory and Practice* is used the world over. Another most useful compilation is *Chromosome Atlas of Flowering Plants of the Indian Subcontinent* (1986), covering 6,973 species, 2,221 enera and 286 families. Banding techniques, chromosome painting, quantification of DNA, *in situ* nucleic acid hybridization and molecular aspects of genome organization are being pursued in India.

Plant Tissue Culture

Plant tissue culture, an off-shoot of human curiosity has presently become an essential component of plant biotechnology. Through the efforts of pioneers in France, USA, U.K. and Germany, plant tissue culture spread to various parts of the world. It was P. Maheshwari who started the first tissue culture Laboratory in India at Delhi University in the 1950s as he foresaw the value of this technique in experimental embryology.

Teachers trained abroad returned to Delhi, Baroda and Pune from where the interest spread to other universitites and CSIR laboratories such as NCL, NBRI, RRL(Jammu), and to BARC, Mumbai. The main benefits erived from tissue culture are: control of organogenesis, elimination of breeding barriers, micropropagation, disease detection and eradication, somatic embryogenesis, use of protoplasts, somatic hybridization, somaclonal variation, detection of genetic variability *in vitro* and production of transgenics. The discovery of androgenic haploidy at Delhi University opened up an entirely new field of research in the production of pure lines of crop plants resulting in reduction of time and labour for exploiting hybrid vigour, especially for rice in China and later for other cereals. Very recently gynogenic haploids have been produced in mulberry.

Undeniably the most useful outcome of tissue culture has been in the micropropagation of ornamentals, agricultural and plantation crops, fruit and forest trees. Laboratory research on micropropagation of plants of economic importance (*Citrus, Eucalyptus*, bamboos, teak, poplar, banana, sugarcane, turmeric and cardamom) has been scaled up to near commercial level. The Asian bamboos have long flowering cycles and come to mast seeding once in 12-120 years. The first demonstration of micropropagation in bamboo using seed callus cultures was done in Delhi and over 10,000 plants were transferred to the field successfully. Several groups working in India and abroad have now demonstrated that micropropagation in bamboos can be accomplished, starting from vegetative parts. The pioneering work done at Delhi and NCL, Pune, led to the discovery that bamboo plantlets can come to flower *in vitro* precociously.

Tissue culture has been effectively used for multiplying and storing economically important, endangered (e.g. *Nepenthes khasiana*), threatened (Himalayan orchids) and biologically incompletely understood plants (Podostemaceae) and medicinal plants (*Dioscorea, Coptis teeta, Valeriana wallichi, Podophyllum hexandrum, Picrorhiza kurroa*) at North-Eastern Hill University (NEHU), DU, NBRI, NCL, ARC, CIMAP and Institute of Himalayan Bioresources and Technology (IHBT), Palampur.

The DBT has established six centres in India to provide hardening facilities for laboratory-raised plants and Micropropagation Technology Parks at TERI and NCL. The National Facility for Plant Tissue Culture Repository (also started by DBT) located at the NBPGR, has now been taken over by the ICAR. Collection, evaluation, introduction, exchange and conservation of germplasm, storage of elite plants, rare hybrids, and germplasm of vegetativelypropagated plants and of plants bearing recalcitrant seeds in the form of tissues or embryonal axes in cryobanks are being practised at NBPGR.

Ecology and Environmental Studies

Plant ecological research in India can be traced to renowned ecologistsÑ R. Misra of Banaras Hindu University (BHU), Varanasi, and F.R. Bharucha of the Institute of Science, Mumbai. Many of the other ecology centres in India owe their origin to persons directly or indirectly trained by Misra. The French Institute (Instit.t Francais) at Pondicherry initiated studies on vegetation cartography in the 1950s. In the beginning yearsattention was paid to the ecology of individual species in the cosystem.

Presently advances have been made in the study of aquatic and wetland ecosystems, marine and mangrove ecosystems. In the study of forest ecosystems focus was shifted to nitrogen budget, mineral recycling, above ground and below ground (fine root) biomass production, functional analysis of effects of changes in land use, phenology of trees and vegetation analysis.

The BHU School has done commendable work on population differentiation, weed ecology, habitat conservation, productivity, energy flow, nutrient cycling and ecology of global change. The ecologists of this school have quantified biomass production and nutrient cycling of pine and oak forests in the Central Himalaya. They have shown that high C : N ratio of litter in pine leads to immobilization of available soil nitrogen, making the habitat inimical to species such as oaks that demand high amounts of nitrogen. This group has carried out detailed analysis of human and forest interactions in the Central Himalaya. The agrosystems in this part of the Himalaya are centres of massive energy consumption and their viability depends on the supply of energy from forests. A significant finding is that these forests are a source of CO_2 rather than a sink. The work on Ganga water was crucial in creating public awareness and inducing public and government participation in the form of Ganga Action Plan. The international journal *Tropical Ecology* was started at BHU and has maintained a high profile, acting as a vehicle to disseminate knowledge generated in and about the tropics.

The ecologists of the French Institute, Pondicherry, in collaboration with the ICAR and State Forest Departments prepared the first vegetation map of Peninsular India in 1956. With the availability of satellite imageries, another project was launched in 973 for the cartography of the forests of the Western Ghats at a scale of 1:25,0000. These maps include details of flora and endemic species in addition to forests, grasslands, and wastelands. Analysis of the maps indicates the percentages of forest cover according to vegetation types. These data coupled with ecological studies in sensitive forest areas have been invaluable in strengthening conservation efforts. Other ecologic aspects studied at the Institute deal with bioclimatology and climate change with reference to deforestation.

Sustained plant ecological work at Rajkot and later at Agra has led to two significant discoveries: *(i)* 25 ecotypes of the desert grass *Cenchrus ciliaris* and nine of *C. setigerus* have been brought to uccessful cultivation in India and America; *(ii)* highest production, perhaps in the country, is in semi-arid areas like Agra Region with fresh or old alluvia, disproving the concept that semi-arid areas are next to arid and vulnerable to desertification (because native vegetation is dominated by C_4 plants with the highest water use efficiency). Several investigators have studied the individual effects of SO_2, fluoride and ozone and particulate matter on plants under controlled conditions at BHU, NBRI and JNU. The combined effects of pollutants ith respect to injury symptoms have also been studied.

The mechanism that prevents toxic effects of heavy metals on the metabolism of cyanobacteria and plants are being studied (BHU). The study of allelo-chemicals released by the weedy species to suppress other plants n the ecosystem has also received recent attention. Bioclimatic studies have beenarried out to correlate vegetation distribution in the origin of tropical evergreen forests. That increasing missions of greenhouse gases, such as CO_2, methane, CFCs, and nitrous oxide, are responsible for global warning is well-established. Among the sources of methane emission India, China and other Asian countries were considered as major contributors with huge areas of rice cultivation. Research carried out by IARI plant physiologists and ecologists at BHU hasclearly indicated that methane emanating from the rice fields is not a major cause of global climate change as claimed by some western scientists.

Much of the ecological research had been carried out as if people did not matter. For the first time in India, a leading plant ecologist and his students began doing ground level research at the NEHU, and subsequently at JNU, in the interphase area of linking ecological and social processes. This group made an interdisciplinary case study of shifting cultivation (*jhum* cultivation) in north-east India, centred around sustainable management of natural resources. The information generated has been synthesized and published in 350 papers and a dozen books. Many traditional societies have accumulated a whole lot of empirical knowledge centred around the economic value of plant and animal species. The main contribution of this group has been to unravel the connection between Traditional Empirical Knowledge (TEK) and natural resource management and landscape management. This work has received international attention. Several strategies have been suggested by them for the improvement of landuse and resource management amongst mountain societies. The Nagaland Experiment of 1976-82 in rural management through Village Development Boards (VDBs) implemented by the government with support from India-Canada Environment Facility, has drawn largely from the research results of the NEHU ecologists.

The political economy of forest resource use has been studied by scientists at the Centre for Ecological Sciences, IISc. This group has brought to light the devastating long-term consequences for short-term gains by state governments. Bamboos were sold to paper mills at a throw-away price of just one rupee per tonne, whereas the basket-weavers had to levy in paying more than Rs. 5,000 per tonne in the Uttra Kannada district of Karnataka. Scientists at this Centre have also studied the ecological History of India and are compiling PeopleÕs Biodiversity Register through participation of schools andcolleges.

The restoration of degraded lands has been studied at BHU and Delhi. An important success story of Delhi University scientists is the rehabilitation of a threestoreyed vegetation in the limestone-mined areas at Bhatta in Mussorie hills and morrum mined-out area of Bhatti wildlife sanctuary in Delhi and extremely desertified land of Asola wildlife sanctuary, using a consortium of microbes belonging to different functional groups, associated with wild legumes and grasses.

Physiology

The rudiments of plant physiology can be traced to pioneers such as J.C. Bose at Calcutta and Dastur in Mumbai. Parija (Cuttack), Sri Ranjan (Allahabad), R.S. Imamdar (BHU), T.Ekambaram (Chennai) and J.C. Sen Gupta (Kolkata) built active schools. The mechanism of regulation of stomatal movements and the various morphological, physiological and biochemical strategies to withstand drought, salinity, alkalinity and cold stress are being investigated (Tirupati, Hyderabad, IARI). Availability of water is a crucial factor that limits crop growth and productivity. With predictions out acute shortage of water in the near future and changing rainfall pattern, plant physiologists are giving serious attention to crop-water relations.

Water Use Efficiency (WUE) is the ratio of the amount of biomass produced over a period of growth to the total amount of water transpired. Scientists at UAS, Bangalore have developed a method of estimating WUE by weighing a large number of plants in containers (mini lysimeters) on a daily basis. There is genotypic variability in WUE. Plants descriminate against heavy isotope of carbon (13C) during photosynthesis. Since intercellular CO_2 concentration determines both carbon isotope descrimination and WUE, a strong inverse correlation exists between these paramters. In genotypes with high WUE, despite high transpiration, mesophyll efficiency for carbon reduction is also high. For rapid screening of genotypes with superior mesophyll efficiency, the Bangalore scientists are using the Isotope Ratio Mass Spectrometer (IRMO, a National facility set up by DST and DBT), which can monitor 13C/12C, 18O/16O , 15N/14N ratios on a continuous flow basis. This set up further facilitates analysis of these traits using molecular markers.

Basic and applied aspects of photosynthesis have been studied by several groups with emphasis on photochemistry, biochemistry and biomass production (JNU, NBRI, MKU, University of Hyderabad). In the mid 1960s the C_4 pathway was discovered in tropical plants which had high productivity. Plant physiologists at IARI noted that in *Sorghum* and *Pennisetum* a change from C_4 to C_3 pathway occurred after flowering. This was the first explanation that C_3 pathway is basic whereas C_4 can change with environment and phenology. Research done at Tirupati showed thatcertain plants are intermediate between C_3 and C_4 in leaf anatomy and biochemistry and also that the same plant may bear leaves with C_3 and C_4 photosynthetic pathway. IARI workers explained that heterosis in yield increment is the culmination of complementary relation between the ÔsourceÕ (foliage) and ÔsinkÕ (grains). The heterosis in height and leaf area are the result of multiplicative effect of their component haracters which show dominance/partial dominance.

Yet another area that has been in the forefront is the understanding of root-shoot signalling as a drought resistance strategy. Signals have been characterized involving the stress hormone abscisic acid (ABA) as a predominant positive signal and ions (calcium, nitrite) and cytokinins as negative signals. Electrical signals are indeed rapid and they can cause closure of stomata in the leaves instantaneously preventing transpiration (UAS, Bangalore). Aschool of mineral nutrition was established at the Lucknow University by S.C. Agarwala to investigate the adequate dosage of micronutrients for important Indian crops and to establish critical limits of deficiency and toxicity. Of special significance is the metabolic and developmental role of micronutrients, especially zinc.

Several groups in India have studied nitrogen metabolism and the regulation of nitrate and nitrite reductase enzymes. Nitrogen fixation by free-living bluegreen algae and other bacteria, and symbiotic prokaryotes has been studied extensively. Pioneers in the area of biological nitrogen fixation are R. N. Singh and G.S. Venkataraman and their students and scientists at Kalyani. The attention of scientists at JNU has been focused on the regulatory aspects of nitrate reductase (NR) in response to light (NR is synthesized in response to phytochrome), hormones, nitrate, ammonium, amino acids and so on. These workers have also shown the phytochrome regulation of Ca+ fluxes and its effects on the turnover of phosphoinositide cycle.

S.M. Sircar and his students at Kolkata were pioneers in India in the physiology of flowering. In later period his group isolated gibberellins from mangroves and water hyacinth. Cytokinins were extracted by other workers from several plants.

According to plant hormone researchers of IISc, Bangalore, cytokinins and auxin are involved in the production of haustoria in the parasitic plant *Cuscuta* even without organic contact with the host. An entirely new group of antigibberellins—the cucurbitacins—which are widespread in the family Cucurbitaceae were reported from Kolkata. Indian scientists have also provided extensive evidence for the growth regulating properties of polyamines. An impressive amount of work has been done on the physiologial effects and agricultural applications of plant growth regulators (PGRs) and their antagonists, especially on the rooting of cuttings, induction of flowering, parthenocarpy, biennial bearing in mango, sex expression, induction of male sterility, defoliation, fruit ripening, and retardation of senescence in flowers. Special mention is made of the work of K.K. Nanda on the induction of flowering in the short day plant (SDP) *Impatiens balsamina* by gibberellins under noninductive conditions and in duckweeds by phenolics, especially salicyclic acid and also by chelating agents at Delhi University.

CONCLUSION

The above account, by no means exhaustive, brings to the fore certain aspects of plant science research in India. From individual efforts with meagre facilities, botanists have proceeded to group activities involving persons from other disciplines. As a humanistic science, botany has begun to embark on areas with deep social concerns. There is still a vast scope for generating new knowledge through basic science to maximize crop yields per unit area, minimize stresses, secure a sured water supply, conserve plant germplasm, cultivate plants that yield products of high economic returns and ensure sustained availability of non-timber forest products to raise the incomes of tribals and the rural poor. What the country needs is a proper blend of nputs from Botany, Microbiology, Agriculture, Chemistry, Forestry, Economics, Sociology and Management.

15

Biological Pest Control

INTRODUCTION

Biological control of pests in agriculture is a method of controlling pests (including insects, mites, weeds and plant diseases) that relies on predation, parasitism, herbivory, or other natural mechanisms. It can be an important component of integrated pest management (IPM) programmes.

Biological control is defined as the reduction of pest populations by natural enemies and typically involves an active human role. Natural enemies of insect pests, also known as biological control agents, include predators, parasitoids, and pathogens. Biological control agents of plant diseases are most often referred to as antagonists. Biological control agents of weeds include herbivores and plant pathogens. Predators, such as lady beetles and lacewings, are mainly free-living species that consume a large number of prey during their lifetime. Parasitoids are species whose immature stage develops on or within a single insect host, ultimately killing the host. Most have a very narrow host range. Many species of wasps and some flies are parasitoids. Pathogens are disease-causing organisms including bacteria, fungi, and viruses. They kill or debilitate their host and are relatively specific to certain insect groups. There are three basic types of biological control strategies; conservation, classical biological control, and augmentation. These are discussed in more detail below.

Conservation

The conservation of natural enemies is probably the most important and readily available biological control practice available to homeowners and gardeners. Natural enemies occur in all areas, from the backyard garden to the commercial field. They are adapted to the local environment and to the target pest, and their conservation is generally simple and cost-effective. Lacewings, lady beetles, hover fly larvae, and parasitized aphid mummies are almost always present in aphid colonies. Fungus-infected adult flies are often common following periods of high humidity. These naturally occurring biological controls are often susceptible to the same pesticides used to target their hosts. Preventing the accidental eradication of natural enemies is termed simple conservation.

Effects of Biological Control on Biodiversity

Biological control can potentially have positive and negative effects on biodiversity. Most of the time a biological control is introduced to an area to protect a native species from an invasive or exotic species that has moved into its area. The control is introduced to lessen the competition among native and invasive species. However, the introduced control does not always target only the intended species. It can also target native species.

When introducing a biological control to a new area, a primary concern is the host- or prey-specificity of the control agent. Generalist feeders (control agents that are not restricted to a single species or a small range of species) often make poor biological control agents, and may become invasive species themselves. For this reason, potential biological control agents should be subject to extensive testing and quarantine before release into any new environment. If a species is introduced and attacks a native species, the biodiversity in that area can decrease dramatically. When one native species is removed from an area, it may have filled an essential niche, When this niche is absent it will directly affect the entire ecosystem. Because they tend to be generalist feeders, vertebrate animals seldom make good biological control agents, and many of the classic cases of "biocontrol gone awry" involve vertebrates. For example, the cane toad (*Bufo marinus*) was introduced as a biological control and had significant negative impact on biodiversity. The cane toad was intentionally introduced to Australia to control the cane beetle. When introduced, the cane toad thrived very well and did not only feed on cane beetles but other insects as well. The cane toad soon spread very rapidly, thus taking over native habitat. The introduction of the cane toad also brought foreign disease to native reptiles. This drastically reduced the population of native toads and frogs. The cane toad also exudes and can squirt poison from the parotid glands on their shoulders when threatened or handled. This toxin contains a cocktail of chemicals that can kill animals that eat it. Freshwater crocodiles, goannas, tiger snakes, dingos and northern quolls have all died after eating cane toads, as have pet dogs. This goes to show a small but deadly organism can alter the native biodiversity in an ecosystem in a very expedient manner. A pyramid effect can take place if native species are reduced or eradicated. The domino effect keeps on going and can potentially exude on other bordering ecosystems until an equilibrium is reached.

A second example of a biological control agent that subsequently crossed over to native species is the *Rhinocyllus conicus*. The seed feeding weevil was introduced to North America to control exotic thistles (Musk and Canadian). However, the weevil did not target only the exotic thistles, it also targeted native thistles that are essential to various native insects. The native insects rely solely on native thistles and do not adapt to other plant species. Therefore, they cannot survive. Biological controls do not always have negative impacts on biodiversity. Successful biological control reduces the density of the target species over several years, thus providing the potential for native species to re-establish. In addition, regeneration and reestablishment programs can aid to the recovery of native species. Native species can be affected in a positive way as well. To develop or find a biological control that exerts control only on the targeted species is a very lengthy process of research and experiments. In the late 1800s, the citrus industry was in great fear when the cottony cushion scale was discovered. This organism could cause a great deal of economic loss to the industry. However, a biological control was introduced. The vedalia beetle and a parasitoid fly were introduced to control the pest. Within a few years time, the cottony cushion scale was controlled by the natural enemies and the citrus industry suffered little financial loss. Many exotic or invasive species can suppress the development of native species. The introduction of an effective biological control that reduces the population of the invasive species allows the rejuvenation of the native species. Biological controls can reduce competition for biotic and abiotic factors which can result in the re-establishment of the once over ran native species

Effects on Invasive Species

The invasive species *Alternanthera philoxeroides* (alligator weed) was successfully controlled in Florida (U.S.) by the introduction of *Agasicles hygrophila* (alligator weed flea beetle).

Invasive species are closely associated with biological controls because the environment in which they are invasive most likely does not contain their natural enemies. If invasive species are not controlled, biodiversity may be at great threat in the affected area. An example of an invasive species is the alligator weed. This plant was introduced to the United States from South America. This aquatic weed spreads very rapidly and causes many problems in lakes and rivers. The weed takes root in shallow water causing major problems such as navigation, irrigation, and flood control. The alligator weed flea beetle and two other biological controls were released in Florida. Because of their success, Florida banned the use of herbicides to control alligator weed three years after the controls were introduced. Biological controls for invasive species also can have a negative impact on biodiversity. The cane toad, as mentioned previously, is a great example of trying to control an invasive species. The cane toad was introduced to eradicate an invasive species. However, it became invasive, thus altering the biodiversity. The introduction of the cane toad could have potentially caused more of a disturbance in biodiversity than the targeted species did.

Effects on Future

With further research and more scientific experiments, biological control could potentially play a huge role in the future of pest prevention. Biological control is being used among society today; however, it could someday reduce the use of many pesticides and herbicides. Since biological control could potentially have a large economic value, if found to be successful, research and job fields would increase continually. By increasing awareness of biological controls among more people, new successful biological controls could be discovered in the future. This could eliminate the overuse of chemicals. Biodiversity would increase because untargeted species that are exterminated with chemicals would no longer occur.

Economic Effects

Therefore, biological control is heavily analyzed by the amount of economic gain that directly comes from biological control. Many of the known economics of biological control are related directly to agriculture practices. Since agriculture has a huge impact on biodiversity this could potentially increase the biodiversity among agricultural practices. In order for agriculture to keep up with the growing population, many inputs are increased resulting in the loss of un-harmful species. Biological control use has been very minimal in agriculture. Less than 1% of global pest control sales of $30 billion involve biological methods. Very few case studies on the cost-benefit analysis of biological control have been done however a few have taken place. A Critical evaluation of augmentative biological control has found four case studies. In one case, "the releases of a parasitoid *Gryon pennsylvanicum* Ashmead to control the true bug *Anasa tristis* DeGeer on pumpkins produced lower net benefit (in dollars) than applications of esfenvalerate (pesticide); 18% lower in one year and 120% lower in the next. In one year of the study, a combination of augmentative releases and use of a resistant pumpkin variety produced greater net benefit than pesticide alone, but not pesticide combined with the resistant variety. Another case study found that "calculated that releases of *T. nubilale* were considerably less cost-effective than pesticide applications used to control ECB on feed corn and fresh-market sweet corn. Pesticide applications produced 87% and 45% more net benefit (in dollars) than augmentation for feed corn and fresh market corn, respectively. In seed corn, however, *Trichogramma* releases produced essentially equivalent net benefits to pesticide treatments. In a third cost-benefit analysis of augmentation, Lundgren et al. (2002) showed that *Trichogramma brassicae* Bezdenko releases produced considerably less net benefit (94%; measured in cabbage head production) than methomyl treatments. In two other studies, "biological control releases were about two times the cost of pesticide applications; this was true for releases of a parasitoid, *Choetospila elegans* Westwood, used to control a stored product pest, *Rhyzopertha dominica* (F.) and releases of green lacewings, *Chrysoperla carnea* Stephens to control leafhoppers in grapes. Finally researchers suggested that *Trichogramma* releases were about six times as expensive as pesticide treatments for *O. nubilalis* in sweet corn,". These case studies offer us some idea of how economical biological control can be. These show that biological control is less cost effective than chemical applications and in result raises a flag that more research needs to be done. With progression in research, we can use more controls at a cheaper cost and increase the amount of biodiversity in areas because of the minimal use of chemicals that cannot target a specific species of pest.

Classical Biological Control

Classical biological control is the introduction of natural enemies to a new locale where they did not originate or do not occur naturally. This is usually done by government authorities. In many instances the complex of natural enemies associated with an insect pest may be inadequate. This is especially evident when an insect pest is accidentally introduced into a new geographic area without its associated natural enemies. These introduced pests are referred to as exotic pests and comprise about 40% of the insect pests in the United States. Examples of introduced vegetable pests include the European corn borer (*Ostrinia nubilalis*), one of the most destructive insects in North America. To obtain the needed natural enemies, scientists turned to classical biological control. This is the practice of importing, and releasing for establishment, natural enemies to control an introduced (exotic) pest, although it is also practiced against native insect pests. The first step in the process is to determine the origin of the introduced pest and then collect appropriate natural enemies associated with the pest or closely related species. The natural enemy is then passed through a rigorous quarantine process, to ensure that no unwanted organisms (such as hyperparasitoids) are introduced, then they are mass produced, and released. Follow-up studies are conducted to determine if the natural enemy becomes successfully established at the site of release, and to assess the long-term benefit of its presence.

There are many examples of successful classical biological control programmes. One of the earliest successes was in controlling *Icerya purchasi*, the cottony cushion scale, a pest that was devastating the California citrus industry in the late 1800s. A predatory insect *Rodolia cardinalis* (the Vedalia Beetle), and a parasitoid fly were introduced from Australia. Within a few years the cottony cushion scale was completely controlled by these introduced natural enemies.

Damage from *Hypera postica* Gyllenhal, the alfalfa weevil, a serious introduced pest of forage, was substantially reduced by the introduction of several natural enemies. About 20 years after their introduction, the population of weevils, in the alfalfa area treated for alfalfa weevil in the Northeastern United States, was reduced by 75 per cent. A small wasp, *Trichogramma ostriniae*, was introduced from China to help control the European corn borer making it a recent example of a long history of classical biological control efforts for this major pest. Many classical biological control programs for insect pests and weeds are under way across the United States and Canada. The population of *Levuana irridescens* (the Levuana moth), a serious coconut pest in Fiji was brought under control by a classical biological control program in the 1920s.

Classical biological control is long lasting and inexpensive. Other than the initial costs of collection, importation, and rearing, little expense is incurred. When a natural enemy is successfully established it rarely requires additional input and it continues to kill the pest with no direct help from humans and at no cost. Unfortunately, classical biological control does not always work. It is usually most effective against exotic pests and less so against native insect pests. The reasons for failure are not often known, but may include the release of too few individuals, poor adaptation of the natural enemy to environmental conditions at the release location, and lack of synchrony between the life cycle of the natural enemy and host pest.

Augmentation

Relatively few natural enemies may be released at a critical time of the season (inoculative release) or literally millions may be released (inundative release). Additionally, the cropping system may be modified to favor or augment the natural enemies. This latter practice is frequently referred to as habitat manipulation. An example of inoculative release occurs in greenhouse production of several crops. Periodic releases of the parasitoid, *Encarsia formosa,* are used to control greenhouse whitefly, and the predaceous mite, *Phytoseiulus persimilis,* is used for control of the two-spotted spider mite. Lady beetles, lacewings, or parasitoids such as those from the genus *Trichogramma* are frequently released in large numbers (inundative release). Recommended release rates for Trichogramma in vegetable or field crops range from 5,000 to 200,000 per acre per week depending on level of pest infestation. Similarly, entomopathogenic nematodes are released at rates of millions and even billions per acre for control of certain soil-dwelling insect pests. A turnaround flowerpot, filled with straw to attract Dermaptera-species. Habitat or environmental manipulation is another form of augmentation. This tactic involves altering the cropping system to augment or enhance the effectiveness of a natural enemy. Many adult parasitoids and predators benefit from sources of nectar and the protection provided by refuges such as hedgerows, cover crops, and weedy borders. Also, the provisioning of natural shelters in the form of wooden caskets, boxes or (turnaround) flowerpots is a form of this. For example, the stimulation of the natural predator *Dermaptera* is done in gardens by hanging up turnaround flowerpots with straw or wood wool.

Mixed plantings and the provision of flowering borders can increase the diversity of habitats and provide shelter and alternative food sources. They are easily incorporated into home gardens and even small-scale commercial plantings, but are more difficult to accommodate in large-scale crop production. There may also be some conflict with pest control for the large producer because of the difficulty of targeting the pest species and the use of refuges by the pest insects as well as natural enemies. Examples of habitat manipulation include growing flowering plants (pollen and nectar sources) near crops to attract and maintain populations of natural enemies. For example, hover fly adults can be attracted to umbelliferous plants in bloom.

Biological control experts in California have demonstrated that planting prune trees in grape vineyards provides an improved overwintering habitat or refuge for a key grape pest parasitoid. The prune trees harbor an alternate host for the parasitoid, which could previously overwinter only at great distances from most vineyards. Caution should be used with this tactic because some plants attractive to natural enemies may also be hosts for certain plant diseases, especially plant viruses that could be vectored by insect pests to the crop. Although the tactic appears to hold much promise, only a few examples have been adequately researched and developed. Lacewings are available from biocontrol dealers.

Ladybugs, and in particular their larvae which are active between May and July in the northern hemisphere, are voracious predators of aphids such as greenfly and blackfly, and will also consume mites, scale insects and small caterpillars. The ladybug is a very familiar beetle with various colored markings, whilst its larvae are initially small and spidery, growing up to 17 mm long. The larvae have a tapering segmented grey/black body with orange/yellow markings and ferocious mouthparts. They can be encouraged by cultivating a patch of nettles in the garden and by leaving hollow stems and some plant debris over winter so that they can hibernate.

Hoverflies resemble slightly darker bees or wasps and they have characteristic hovering, darting flight patterns. There are over 100 species of hoverfly whose larvae principally feed upon greenfly, one larva devouring up to fifty a day, or 1000 in its lifetime. They also eat fruit tree spider mites and small caterpillars. Adults feed on nectar and pollen, which they require for egg production. Eggs are minute (1 mm), pale yellow white and laid singly near greenfly colonies. Larvae are 8-17 mm long, disguised to resemble bird droppings, they are legless and have no distinct head. Semi-transparent in a range of colours from green, white, brown and black.

Hoverflies can be encouraged by growing attractant flowers such as the poached egg plant *(Limnanthes douglasii)*, marigolds or phacelia throughout the growing season.

Dragonflies are important predators of mosquitoes, both in the water, where the dragonfly naiads eat mosquito larvae, and in the air, where adult dragonflies capture and eat adult mosquitoes. Community-wide mosquito control programs that spray adult mosquitoes also kill dragonflies, thus removing an important biocontrol agent, and can actually increase mosquito populations in the long term.

Other useful garden predators include lacewings, pirate bugs, rove and ground beetles, aphid midge, centipedes, predatory mites, as well as larger fauna such as frogs, toads, lizards, hedgehogs, slow-worms and birds. Cats and rat terriers kill field mice, rats, June bugs, and birds. Dogs chase away many types of pest animals. Dachshunds are bred specifically to fit inside tunnels underground to kill badgers.

- *Phytoseiulus persimilis* (against spider mites)
- *Amblyseius californicus* (against spider mites)
- *Amblyseius cucumeris* (against spider mites) *Typhlodromips swirskii* (against spider mites, thrips, and white flies)
- *Feltiella acarisuga* (against spider mites)
- *Stethorus punctillum* (against spider mites)
- *Macrolophus caluginosus* (against spider mites)
- *Encarsia formosa* (against white flies)
- *Eretmocerus* spp. (against white flies

Directly Introducing Biological Controls

Most of the biological controls listed above depend on providing incentives in order to 'naturally' attract beneficial insects to the garden. However there are occasions when biological controls can be directly introduced. Common biocontrol agents include parasitoids, predators, pathogens or weed feeders. This is particularly appropriate in situations such as the greenhouse, a largely artificial environment, and are usually purchased by mail order.

Some biocontrol agents that can be introduced include:

- *Encarsia formosa*. This is a small predatory chalcid wasp which is parasitical on whitefly, a sap-feeding insect which can cause wilting and black sooty moulds. It is most effective when dealing with low level infestations, giving protection over a long period of time. The wasp lays its eggs in young whitefly 'scales', turning them black as the parasite larvae pupates. It should be introduced as soon as possible after the first adult whitefly are seen. Should be used in conjunction with insecticidal soap.
- Red spider mite, another pest found in the greenhouse, can be controlled with the predatory mite *Phytoseilus persimilis*. This is slightly larger than its prey and has an orange body. It develops from egg to adult twice as fast as the red spider mite and once established quickly overcomes infestation.
- A fairly recent development in the control of slugs is the introduction of 'Nemaslug', a microscopic nematode (*Phasmarhabditis hermaphrodita*) which will seek out and parasitize slugs, reproducing inside them and killing them. The nematode is applied by watering onto moist soil, and gives protection for up to six weeks in optimum conditions, though is mainly effective with small and young slugs under the soil surface.
- A bacterial biological control which can be introduced in order to control butterfly caterpillars is *Bacillus thuringiensis*. This available in sachets of dried spores which are mixed with water and sprayed onto vulnerable plants

such as brassicas and fruit trees. The bacterial disease will kill the caterpillars, but leave other insects unharmed. There are strains of *Bt* that are effective against other insect larvae. *Bt israelensis* is effective against mosquito larvae and some midges.

The European Rabbit (*Oryctolagus cuniculus*) is seen as a major pest in Australia

- A viral biological control which can be introduced in order to control the overpopulation of European rabbit in Australia is the rabbit haemorrhagic disease virus that causes the rabbit haemorrhagic disease.
- A biological control being developed for use in the treatment of plant disease is the fungus *Trichoderma viride*. This has been used against Dutch Elm disease, and to treat the spread of fungal and bacterial growth on tree wounds. It may also have potential as a means of combating silver leaf disease.

The parasitoid *Gonatocerus ashmeadi* (Hymenoptera: Mymaridae) has been introduced to control the glassy-winged sharpshooter *Homalodisca vitripennis* (Hemipterae: Cicadellidae) in French Polynesia and has successfully controlled ~95% of the pest density.

16

Plant Kingdom and Plant Genetics

Introduction

Plant Taxonomy

Plant Kingdom has about 260,000 species divided into two phyla (or divisions in plants):

1. ***Bryophyta*** (*non-vascular plants, lower plants*): They lack a vascular system for the internal conduction of water, minerals and food (lower plants), and depend on direct contact with surface water. This group includes mosses, liverworts and hornworts. There is always an alternation of generations between morphologically distinct sporophyte and gametophyte. The familiar leafy plant of Bryophytes is the sexual, gamete-producing (gametophyte) generation of their life cycle.

2. ***Tracheophyta*** (*vascular plants, higher plants*): This group consists of plants that have a vascular system, i.e., xylem and phloem (water/mineral and food-conducting tissues, respectively). Tracheophyte leafy plants are the asexual, spore-producing, diploid (sporophyte) generation of their life cycle. One Subphylum, Pteropsida, consists of the following superclasses:

(i) ***Filinicae Ferns.*** They do not reproduce by seeds but by spores like the Phylum Bryophyta. Alternation of generation is typical of ferns and Bryophyta.

(ii) ***Gymnosperms:*** Cone-bearing woody seed plants. Includes cycads, gingko, **conifers** (pines, cedars) and gnetophytes.

(iii) ***Angiosperms:*** Flower plants (divides into monocots and dicots). The gymnosperms and angiosperms are collectively called Spermatophyte (seed-bearing) plants. In this group, the gametophyte (haploid) generation does not occur as an independent plant (as in ferns). The vestigial gametophytes are contained in the sporophyte tissue as a few nuclei and can only be seen by a microscope (the embryonic sac and the pollen grain). The sporophyte embryo is contained in a seed which is dispersed from the plant. The angiosperms, therefore, cannot produce asexual spores and there is no obvious alternation of generations. The haploid pollen and ovule produced by a flower are thought to contain the remains of the gametophyte generation which was typical of the ancestors of the angiosperms (up to and including ferns). Link to Plant Evolution and Classification in Kimball's Biology Pages.

Plant Evolution

Evolution of eukaryotes from a presumed bacteria-like ancestor is one of the major events in evolutionary history. They have a distinct nucleus, organelles involved in energy metabolism (mitochondria and chloroplast), extensive internal membranes and a cytoskeleton of protein fibres and flaments. Chloroplasts (photosynthesis) in green plants and algae originated as free living bacteria related to the cyanobacteria [the chloroplastic DNA is more similar to free-living Cyanobacteria DNA than to sequences from the plants the chloroplasts reside in]. The eukaryotic mitochondria (ATP synthesis) are endosymbionts like chloroplasts. Mitochondria were acquired when aerobic Eubacteria were engulfed by anaerobic host cells. As they conferred useful functions like aerobic respiration (mitochondria) and photosynthesis (chloroplasts), these organelles have been retained as endosymbionts. This must have happened after the nucleus was acquired by the eukaryotic lineage. The origin of eukaryotic nucleus is almost certainly autogenous and not a result of endosymbiosis. Mitochondria are believed to have originated not from cyanobacteria but from an ancestor of the present-day purple photosynthetic bacteria that had lost its capacity for photosynthesis (chloroplasts from an ancestral Cyanobacterium).

All land plants evolved from the green algae or Chlorophyta. In the period before the Permian (the Carboniferous), the landscape was dominated by seedless ferns and their relatives. Vascular plants first appeared in Silurian (439-409 Mya). After the Permian extinction, gymnosperms became more abundant. They evolved seeds and pollens (encased sperm). Angiosperms evolved from gymnosperms during the early Cretaceous about 140-125 Mya. They further diversified and dispersed during the late Cretaceous (97.5-66.5 Mya). Water lilies are one of the most ancient angiosperm plants. Currently, over three quarters of all living plants are angiosperms. The angiosperms developed a close contact with insects which promoted cross-pollination and resulted in more vigorous offspring. Their generation time to reproduce is short, and their seeds can be dispersed by animals. For these reasons, the angiosperms were able to travel and disperse all around the world. The important events in the evolution of the angiosperms were the evolution of showy flowers (to attract insects and birds), the evolution of bilaterally symmetrical flowers (adaptation for specialized pollinators), and the evolution of larger and more mobile animals (to disperse fruits and seeds).

Polyploidy is an important mechanism in the evolution of plants. It is a situation in which the organism has more than two (2n) sets of chromosomes. It can be 3n, 4n or more. A high proportion (47%) of angiosperms are polyploid. It arises as a result of meiotic irregularities and results in sterile progeny which can still reproduce asexually. The original South American potato is a tetraploid (4n). Many of the common food plants (strawberries, apples, potatoes) are polyploid as this results in larger flowers and fruits (as well as larger cells, thicker and fleshier leaves). The wheat now grown for bread (*T. aestivum*) is hexaploid (6n = 42 chromosomes). Polyploidy can be induced by treatment of colchicines experimentally. Triploid offspring can be produced by crossing a colchicine-induced or naturally occurring tetraploid and a diploid. Odd number polyploids are sterile because they cannot segregate chromosomes evenly into gametes in meiosis. Sterility caused by triploidy is useful to produce seedless fruit that is easier to eat (banana) or better tasting (less bitter cucumbers). Polyploidy is a common mechanism for sympatric speciation (reproductive isolation without geographical isolation).

PLANT BIOLOGY

Plants are eukaryotic, multicellular organisms. A plant cell differs from an animal cell in that they have rigid cell walls composed of cellulose, chlorophyll containing plastids (chloroplasts), and are able to photosyntesize. Fungi are different because they lack chlorophyll and chloroplasts, their cell walls contain chitin. Algae were formerly thought to be plants because of their rigid cell wall and photosynthesizing ability. They are, however, currently placed in the Kingdom Protoctista because of the variety of cell pigments, cell wall types and different forms and structures.

Plant Reproduction

Asexual reproduction: Potato (tubers), strawberry (runners), iris (rhizomes) and gladiolus (corms) are common examples.

Sexual reproduction: Because land plants are immobile, alternation of generations has evolved in some groups to allow fertilization. The plants that possess leaves, roots, stems and flowers are sporophytes (asexually reproducing). This generation gives rise to the gametophyte generation (sexually reproducing). One spore type (microspore) develops into a male gametophyte and the other kind (megaspore) into a female gametophyte. The female gametophyte remains protected in the carpel of the flower. When fertilized, an embryo is formed (a seed) which is a young sporophyte able to form a new organism when germinated.

The female gametophyte (ovum) of a flowering plant is formed in the ovules at the centre of the flower. After meiosis, an embryo sac forms (this is the female gametophyte generation of the alternation of generations in flowering plants). This consists of the ovum and several other haploid cells. The male gametophyte is the pollen grain. Two haploid sperm are produced in each pollen grain. The pollen grain should reach to the stigma of the recipient -female- flower. Following pollination, it germinates and a pollen tube grows down into the ovule carrying the two nonmotile sperm. One of these fuses with the ovum to form a zygote while the other fuses with two other cells of the embryo sac to form a triploid nutritive tissue called endosperm. This is called double fertilization and is unique to plants. The zygote divides to give rise to two cells. One will form the embryo and the other a supportive structure (suspensor). Embryonic differentiation starts but does not proceed for long. When the development ceases, the embryo becomes packaged in a seed, specialized for dispersal.

Pollination: This can be achieved via self-pollination (autogamy) or cross-pollination (allogamy). Most plants reproduce by both self and cross-pollination. Cross-pollinating plants produce better-quality seeds and more varied (adaptable) offspring. Because of the advantages of cross-pollination, most plants have evolved mechanisms to prevent self-pollination. One of them is production of some chemicals that prevent pollen from growing on the stigma of the same flower, or from developing the pollen tubes in the style (self-incompatibility system). Some plants produce only one kind of (either male or female) flowers (dioecious) and some are dichogamous (the two separate sex organs develop at different times in the same flower: protandry or protogyny). Cross-pollination can be achieved by wind, insects (honey bee), bats and birds. One feature that developed as a result of insect pollination is pollen-tube competition. When a number of pollen grains is deposited on a stigma, each pollen grows a pollen tube to reach the ovule. Whichever reaches first, it fertilizes the ovule. The fastest growing pollen tube usually carries the best genes and results in a more vigorous offspring. Therefore, apart from avoidance of self-fertilization, there is selection for the best cross-pollinating pollen as well (sexual selection in plants).

Unique Genetic Features of Plants

- Ability to photosynthesize
- Totipotency of plant cells
- Hermaphroditism and ability to reproduce both sexually and asexually
- Double fertilization
- Polyploidy
- Alternation of generations
- Mitosis in haploid state

Agricultural Biotechnology

To create plants with altered characters, gene transfer has been used extensively in recent years. In principle, it is the same procedure as used in other organisms. Plants are especially suitable for genetic modification because most plant cells are totipotent. This means that a plant can be generated from a single genetically modified cell (i.e., it would not require fertilization). The most commonly used carrier vector in plant genetic modification is the Ti plasmid of Agrobacterium tumefaciens. The 30 kb-long T-DNA part of this plasmid is able to integrate into plant chromosomes. This plasmid can be used to transfer up to 40 kb inserted DNA into a protoplast (a plant cell whose cell wall has been destroyed enzymatically). The engineered protoplast has the ability to act as a (fertilized) germ cell and to regenerate into a whole plant (totipotency). An alternative gene transfer method for plant cells is penetrating the cells with DNA coated gold and tungsten spheres fired from a special gun (this technique is called biolistics). The common purposes of genetic modification in plants are induction of resistance to insects, viruses, herbicides and commercial benefit (such as higher yield, seedless fruits, long-lasting tomatoes). Plants can also be used as bioreactors to produce desired recombinant proteins.

17

Importance of Plants

INTRODUCTION

Plants are living organisms belonging to the kingdom Plantae. They include familiar organisms such as trees, herbs, bushes, grasses, vines, ferns, mosses, and green algae. About 350,000 species of plants, defined as seed plants, bryophytes, ferns and fern allies, are estimated to exist currently. As of 2004, some 287,655 species had been identified, of which 258,650 are flowering and 18,000 bryophytes. Green plants, sometimes called metaphytes or *viridiplantae*, obtain most of their energy from sunlight via a process called photosynthesis.

Aristotle divided all living things between plants (which generally do not move), and animals (which often are mobile to catch their food). In Linnaeus' system, these became the Kingdoms Vegetabilia (later Metaphyta or Plantae) and Animalia (also called Metazoa). Since then, it has become clear that the Plantae as originally defined included several unrelated groups, and the fungi and several groups of algae were removed to new kingdoms. However, these are still often considered plants in many contexts, both technical and popular.

When the name Plantae or plants is applied to a specific taxon, it is usually referring to one of three concepts. From smallest to largest in inclusiveness, these three groupings are:

- Land plants, also known as Embryophyta or Metaphyta. As the narrowest of plant categories, this is further delineated below.
- Green plants - also known as Viridiplantae, Viridiphyta or Chlorobionta - comprise the above Embryophytes, Charophyta (i.e., primitive stoneworts), and Chlorophyta (i.e., green algae such as sea lettuce). It is this clade which is mainly the subject of this article.
- Archaeplastida - also known as Plantae *sensu lato*, Plastida or Primoplantae - comprises the green plants above, as well as Rhodophyta (red algae) and Glaucophyta (simple glaucophyte algae). As the broadest plant clade, this comprises most of the eukaryotes that eons ago acquired their chloroplasts directly by engulfing cyanobacteria.

Informally, other creatures that carry out photosynthesis are called plants as well, but they do not constitute a formal taxon and represent species that are not closely related to true plants. There are around 375,000 species of plants, and each year more are found and described by science.

Algae

Most algae are no longer classified within the Kingdom Plantae the algae comprise several different groups of organisms that produce energy through photosynthesis, each of which arose independently from separate non-photosynthetic ancestors. Most conspicuous among the algae are the seaweeds, multicellular algae that may roughly resemble terrestrial plants, but are classified among the green, red, and brown algae. Each of these algal groups also includes various microscopic and single-celled organisms.

Only two groups of algae are considered close relatives of land plants (embryophytes). The first of these groups is the Charophyta (desmids and stoneworts), from which the embryophytes developed. The sister group to the combined embryophytes and charophytes is the other group of green algae (Chlorophyta), and this more inclusive group is collectively referred to as the green plants or Viridiplantae. The Kingdom

Plantae is often taken to mean this monophyletic grouping. With a few exceptions among the green algae, all such forms have cell walls containing cellulose, have chloroplasts containing chlorophylls *a* and *b*, and store food in the form of starch. They undergo closed mitosis without centrioles, and typically have mitochondria with flat cristae.

The chloroplasts of green plants are surrounded by two membranes, suggesting they originated directly from endosymbiotic cyanobacteria. The same is true of two additional groups of algae: the Rhodophyta (red algae) and Glaucophyta. All three groups together are generally believed to have a common origin, and so are classified together in the taxon Archaeplastida. In contrast, most other algae (e.g. heterokonts, haptophytes, dinoflagellates, and euglenids) have chloroplasts with three or four surrounding membranes. They are not close relatives of the green plants, presumably acquiring chloroplasts separately from ingested or symbiotic green and red algae.

Fungi

Fungi were previously included in the plant kingdom, but are now seen to be more closely related to animals. Unlike embryophytes and algae, fungi are not photosynthetic, but are saprotrophs: obtaining food by breaking down and absorbing surrounding materials. Most fungi are formed by microscopic structures called hyphae, which may or may not be divided into cells but contain eukaryotic nuclei. Fruiting bodies, of which mushrooms are most familiar, are the reproductive structures of fungi. They are not related to any of the photosynthetic groups, but are close relatives of animals. Therefore, the fungi are in a kingdom of their own.

Embryophytes

Most familiar are the multicellular land plants, called embryophytes. They include the vascular plants, plants with full systems of leaves, stems, and roots. They also include a few of their close relatives, often called *bryophytes*, of which mosses and liverworts are the most common.

All of these plants have eukaryotic cells with cell walls composed of cellulose, and most obtain their energy through photosynthesis, using light and carbon dioxide to synthesize food. About three hundred plant species do not photosynthesize but are parasites on other species of photosynthetic plants. Plants are distinguished from green algae, which represent a mode of photosynthetic life similar to the kind modern plants are believed to have evolved from, by having specialized reproductive organs protected by non-reproductive tissues.

Bryophytes first appeared during the early Palaeozoic. They can only survive where moisture is available for significant periods, although some species are desiccation tolerant. Most species of bryophyte remain small throughout their life-cycle. This involves an alternation between two generations: a haploid stage, called the gametophyte, and a diploid stage, called the sporophyte. The sporophyte is short-lived and remains dependent on its parent gametophyte. Vascular plants first appeared during the Silurian period, and by the Devonian had diversified and spread into many different land environments. They have a number of adaptations that allowed them to overcome the limitations of the bryophytes. These include a cuticle resistant to desiccation, and vascular tissues which transport water throughout the organism. In most the sporophyte acts as a separate individual, while the gametophyte remains small.

The first primitive seed plants, Pteridosperms (seed ferns) and Cordaites, both groups now extinct, appeared in the late Devonian and diversified through the Carboniferous, with further evolution through the Permian and Triassic periods. In these the gametophyte stage is completely reduced, and the sporophyte begins life inside an enclosure called a seed, which develops while on the parent plant, and with fertilisation by means of pollen grains. Whereas other vascular plants, such as ferns, reproduce by means of spores and so need moisture to develop, some seed plants can survive and reproduce in extremely arid conditions.

Early seed plants are referred to as gymnosperms (naked seeds), as the seed embryo is not enclosed in a protective structure at pollination, with the pollen landing directly on the embryo. Four surviving groups remain widespread now, particularly the conifers, which are dominant trees in several biomes. The angiosperms, comprising the flowering plants, were the last major group of plants to appear, emerging from within the gymnosperms during the Jurassic and diversifying rapidly during the Cretaceous. These differ in that the seed embryo (angiosperm) is enclosed, so the pollen has to grow a tube to penetrate the protective seed coat; they are the predominant group of flora in most biomes today.

Fossils

Plant fossils include roots, wood, leaves, seeds, fruit, pollen, spores, phytoliths, and amber (the fossilized resin produced by some plants). Fossil land plants are recorded in terrestrial, lacustrine, fluvial and nearshore marine sediments. Pollen, spores and algae (dinoflagellates and acritarchs) are used for dating sedimentary rock sequences. The remains of fossil plants are not as common as fossil animals, although plant fossils are locally abundant in many regions worldwide. The earliest fossils clearly assignable to Kingdom Plantae are fossil green algae from the Cambrian. These fossils resemble calcified multicellular members of the Dasycladales. Earlier Precambrian fossils are known which resemble single-cell green algae, but definitive identity with that group of algae is uncertain. The oldest known trace fossils of embryophytes date from the Ordovician, though such fossils are fragmentary. By the Silurian, fossils of whole plants are preserved, including the lycophyte *Baragwanathia longifolia*. From the Devonian, detailed fossils of rhyniophytes have been found. Early fossils of these ancient plants show the individual cells within the plant tissue. The Devonian period also saw the evolution of what many believe to be the first modern tree, *Archaeopteris*. This fern-like tree combined a woody trunk with the fronds of a fern, but produced no seeds.

The Coal Measures are a major source of Palaeozoic plant fossils, with many groups of plants in existence at this time. The spoil heaps of coal mines are the best places to collect; coal itself is the remains of fossilised plants, though structural detail of the plant fossils is rarely visible in coal. In the Fossil Forest at Victoria Park in Glasgow, Scotland, the stumps of *Lepidodendron* trees are found in their original growth positions. The fossilized remains of conifer and angiosperm roots, stems and branches may be locally abundant in lake and inshore sedimentary rocks from the Mesozoic and Caenozoic eras. Sequoia and its allies, magnolia, oak, and palms are often found. Petrified wood is common in some parts of the world, and is most frequently found in arid or desert areas where it is more readily exposed by erosion. Petrified wood is often heavily silicified (the organic material replaced by silicon dioxide), and the impregnated tissue is often preserved in fine detail. Such specimens may be cut and polished using lapidary equipment. Fossil forests of petrified wood have been found in all continents. Fossils of seed ferns such as *Glossopteris* are widely distributed throughout several continents of the southern hemisphere, a fact that gave support to Alfred Wegener's early ideas regarding Continental drift theory.

LIFE PROCESSES

Growth

Most of the solid material in a plant is taken from the atmosphere. Through a process known as photosynthesis, plants use the energy in sunlight to convert carbon dioxide from the atmosphere, plus water, into simple sugars. These sugars are then used as building blocks and form the main structural component of the plant. Chlorophyll, a green-colored, magnesium-containing pigment is essential to this process; it is generally present in plant leaves, and often in other plant parts as well. Plants rely on soil primarily for support and water (in quantitative terms), but also obtain compounds of nitrogen, phosphorus, and other crucial elemental nutrients. For the majority of plants to grow successfully they also require oxygen in the atmosphere and around their roots for respiration. However, some plants grow as submerged aquatics, using oxygen dissolved in the surrounding water, and a few specialized vascular plants, such as mangroves, can grow with their roots in anoxic conditions. The leaf is the primary site of photosynthesis in plants.

Factors Affecting Growth

The genotype of a plant affects its growth, for example selected varieties of wheat grow rapidly, maturing within 110 days, whereas others, in the same environmental conditions, grow more slowly and mature within 155 days. Growth is also determined by environmental factors, such as temperature, available water, available light, and available nutrients in the soil. Any change in the availability of these external conditions will be reflected in the plants growth. Biotic factors (living organisms) also affect plant growth.

- Plants compete with other plants for space, water, light and nutrients. Plants can be so crowded that no single individual makes normal growth.
- Many plants rely on birds and insects to effect pollination.
- Grazing animals may affect vegetation.
- Soil fertility is influenced by the activity of bacteria and fungi.
- Bacteria, fungi, viruses, nematodes and insects can parasitise plants.
- Some plant roots require an association with fungi to maintain normal activity (mycorrhizal association).

Simple plants like algae may have short life spans as individuals, but their populations are commonly seasonal. Other plants may be organized according to their seasonal growth pattern:

- *Annual:* live and reproduce within one growing season.
- *Biennial:* live for two growing seasons; usually reproduce in second year.
- *Perennial:* live for many growing seasons; continue to reproduce once mature.

Among the vascular plants, perennials include both evergreens that keep their leaves the entire year, and deciduous plants which lose their leaves for some part of it. In temperate and boreal climates, they generally lose their leaves during the winter; many tropical plants lose their leaves during the dry season. The growth rate of plants is extremely variable. Some mosses grow less than 0.001 mm/h, while most trees grow 0.025-0.250 mm/h. Some climbing species, such as kudzu, which do not need to produce thick supportive tissue, may grow up to 12.5 mm/h. Plants protect themselves from frost and dehydration stress with antifreeze proteins, heat-shock proteins and sugars (sucrose is common). LEA (Late Embryogenesis Abundant) protein expression is induced by stresses and protects other proteins from aggregation as a result of desiccation and freezing.

Internal Distribution

Vascular plants differ from other plants in that they transport nutrients between different parts through specialized structures, called xylem and phloem. They also have roots for taking up water and minerals. The xylem moves water and minerals from the root to the rest of the plant, and the phloem provides the roots with sugars and other nutrient produced by the leaves.

Ecology

The photosynthesis conducted by land plants and algae is the ultimate source of energy and organic material in nearly all ecosystems. Photosynthesis radically changed the composition of the early Earth's atmosphere, which as a result is now 21% oxygen. Animals and most other organisms are aerobic, relying on oxygen; those that do not are confined to relatively rare anaerobic environments. Plants are the primary producers in most terrestrial ecosystems and form the basis of the food web in those ecosystems. Many animals rely on plants for shelter as well as oxygen and food. Land plants are key components of the water cycle and several other biogeochemical cycles. Some plants have coevolved with nitrogen fixing bacteria, making plants an important part of the nitrogen cycle. Plant roots play an essential role in soil development and prevention of soil erosion.

Ecological Relationships

Numerous animals have coevolved with plants. Many animals pollinate flowers in exchange for food in the form of pollen or nectar. Many animals disperse seeds, often by eating fruit and passing the seeds in their feces. Myrmecophytes are plants that have coevolved with ants. The plant provides a home, and sometimes food, for the ants. In exchange, the ants defend the plant from herbivores and sometimes competing plants. Ant wastes provide organic fertilizer. The majority of plant species have various kinds of fungi associated with their root systems in a kind of mutualistic symbiosis known as mycorrhiza.

The fungi help the plants gain water and mineral nutrients from the soil, while the plant gives the fungi carbohydrates manufactured in photosynthesis. Some plants serve as homes for endophytic fungi that protect the plant from herbivores by producing toxins. The fungal endophyte, *Neotyphodium coenophialum*, in tall fescue (*Festuca arundinacea*) does tremendous economic damage to the cattle industry in the U.S. Various forms of parasitism are also fairly common among plants, from the semi-parasitic mistletoe that merely takes some nutrients from its host, but still has photosynthetic leaves, to the fully parasitic broomrape and toothwort that acquire all their nutrients through connections to the roots of other plants, and so have no chlorophyll. Some plants, known as myco-heterotrophs, parasitize mycorrhizal fungi, and hence act as epiparasites on other plants.

Many plants are epiphytes, meaning they grow on other plants, usually trees, without parasitizing them. Epiphytes may indirectly harm their host plant by intercepting mineral nutrients and light that the host would otherwise receive. The weight of large numbers of epiphytes may break tree limbs. Many orchids, bromeliads, ferns and mosses often grow as epiphytes. Bromeliad epiphytes accumulate water in leaf axils to form phytotelmata, complex aquatic food webs. A few plants are carnivorous, such as the Venus flytrap and sundew. They trap small animals and digest them to obtain mineral nutrients, especially nitrogen.

Importance

Potato Plant

Potatoes spread to the rest of the world after European contact with the Americas in the late 1400s and early 1500s and have since become an important field crop.

The study of plant uses by people is termed economic botany or ethnobotany. They are often used as synonyms but some consider economic botany to focus mainly on uses of modern cultivated plants, while ethnobotany studies uses of indigenous plants by native peoples. Human cultivation of plants is part of agriculture, which is the basis of human civilization. Plant agriculture is subdivided into agronomy, horticulture and forestry.

Food

Virtually all human nutrition depends on land plants directly or indirectly. Much of human nutrition depends on cereals, especially maize or corn, wheat and rice or other staple crops such as potato, cassava, and legumes. Other parts from plants that are eaten include fruits, vegetables, nuts, herbs, spices and edible flowers. Beverages from plants include coffee, tea, wine, beer and alcohol. Sugar is obtained mainly from sugar cane and sugar beet. Cooking oils and margarine come from corn, soybean, canola, safflower, sunflower, olive and others. Food additives include gum arabic, guar gum, locust bean gum, starch and pectin.

Nonfood Products

Wood is used for buildings, furniture, paper, cardboard, musical instruments and sports equipment. Cloth is often made from cotton, flax or synthetic fibers derived from cellulose, such as rayon and acetate. Renewable fuels from plants include firewood, peat and many other biofuels. Coal and petroleum are fossil fuels derived from plants. Medicines derived from plants include aspirin, taxol, morphine, quinine, reserpine, colchicine, digitalis and vincristine. There are hundreds of herbal supplements such as ginkgo, Echinacea, feverfew, and Saint John's wort. Pesticides derived from plants include nicotine, rotenone, strychnine and pyrethrins. Drugs obtained from plants include opium, cocaine and marijuana. Poisons from plants include ricin, hemlock and curare. Plants are the source of many natural products such as fibers, essential oils, dyes, pigments, waxes, tannins, latex, gums, resins, alkaloids, amber and cork.

Products derived from plants include soaps, paints, shampoos, perfumes, cosmetics, turpentine, rubber, varnish, lubricants, linoleum, plastics, inks, chewing gum and hemp rope. Plants are also a primary source of basic chemicals for the industrial synthesis of a vast array of organic chemicals. These chemicals are used in a vast variety of studies and experiments.

Aesthetic Uses

Thousands of plant species are cultivated to beautify the human environment as well as to provide shade, modify temperatures, reduce windspeed, abate noise, provide privacy and prevent soil erosion. People use cut flowers, dried flowers and house plants indoors. Outdoors, they use lawn grasses, shade trees, ornamental trees, shrubs, vines, herbaceous perennials and bedding plants. Images of plants are often used in art, architecture, humor, language and photography and on textiles, money, stamps, flags and coats of arms. Living plant art forms include topiary, bonsai, ikebana and espalier. Ornamental plants have sometimes changed the course of history, as in tulipomania. Plants are the basis of a multi-billion dollar per year tourism industry which includes travel to arboretums, botanical gardens, historic gardens, national parks, tulip festivals, rainforests, forests with colorful autumn leaves and the National Cherry Blossom Festival. Venus flytrap, sensitive plant and resurrection plant are examples of plants sold as novelties.

Scientific and Cultural Uses

Tree rings are an important method of dating in archeology and serve as a record of past climates. Basic biological research has often been done with plants, such as the pea plants used to derive Gregor Mendel's laws of genetics. Space stations or space colonies may one day rely on plants for life support. Plants are used as national and state emblems, including state trees and state flowers. Ancient trees are revered and many are famous. Numerous world records are held by plants. Plants are often used as memorials, gifts and to mark special occasions such as births, deaths, weddings and holidays. Plants figure prominently in mythology, religion and literature. The field of ethnobotany studies plant use by indigenous cultures which helps to conserve endangered species as well as discover new medicinal plants. Gardening is the most popular leisure activity in the U.S. Working with plants or horticulture therapy is beneficial for rehabilitating people with disabilities. Certain plants contain psychotropic chemicals which are extracted and ingested, including tobacco, cannabis (marijuana), and opium.

Negative Effects

Weeds are plants that grow where people do not want them. People have spread plants beyond their native ranges and some of these introduced plants become invasive, damaging existing ecosystems by displacing native species. Invasive plants cause billions of dollars in crop losses annually by displacing crop plants, they increase the cost of production and the use of chemical means to control them affects the environment.

Plants may cause harm to people. Plants that produce windblown pollen invoke allergic reactions in people who suffer from hay fever. A wide variety of plants are poisonous. Several plants cause skin irritations when touched, such as poison ivy. Certain plants contain psychotropic chemicals, which are extracted and ingested or smoked, including tobacco, cannabis (marijuana), cocaine and opium, causing damage to health or even death Both illegal and legal drugs derived from plants have negative effects on the economy, affecting worker productivity and law enforcement costs. Some plants cause allergic reactions in people and animals when ingested, while other plants cause food intolerances that negatively affect health.

Index

C

D

E

F

G

H

I

Q

R

S

T

❑❑❑